BLOOD
AND
IRON

BLOOD
AND
IRON

THE RISE AND FALL OF THE GERMAN EMPIRE

1871–1918

KATJA HOYER

PEGASUS BOOKS
NEW YORK LONDON

BLOOD AND IRON

Pegasus Books, Ltd.
148 West 37th Street, 13th Floor
New York, NY 10018

Copyright © 2021 by Katja Hoyer

First Pegasus Books paperback edition November 2022
First Pegasus Books cloth edition December 2021

ISBN: 978-1-63936-297-4

10 9 8 7 6 5 4 3 2

Printed in the United States of America
Distributed by Simon & Schuster
www.pegasusbooks.com

CONTENTS

INTRODUCTION

On the bright, cold winter morning of 17 January 1871, Wilhelm I, King of Prussia, had a moment of crisis. Eventually, the old man lost what self-control he still had and began to sob, 'Tomorrow will be the unhappiest day of my life! We are going to witness the burial of the Prussian monarchy and this, Count Bismarck, is all your fault!' The 73-year-old king was an unlikely candidate to assume the mantle of the mystical Kaiser who would arise one day to unite all Germans. Yet this was precisely what was now expected of him. The next day, on 18 January 1871, around noon, several hundred Prussian officers, members of the nobility and representatives of all the German regiments that had fought in the Franco-Prussian War gathered in the Hall of Mirrors of the Palace of Versailles. The sound of marching bands drifted into the magnificent room through the tall windows and mingled with the excited chatter of the waiting crowds. Then the large double-doors at the end of the dazzling hall opened, and Wilhelm I, Crown Prince Friedrich and the representatives of the German states entered in a ceremonial procession. A strained, expectant silence fell. There was a sense that those present were witnessing a historical moment, one of mythical proportions.

Wilhelm had managed to pull himself together and stiffly accepted the title that was offered to him formally by the German princes during the ceremony. And yet there was already a sense that the journey ahead would not be easy for the newly formed nation. At its helm would be a monarch who had refused the title 'German Kaiser' and only reluctantly accepted the more neutral 'Kaiser Wilhelm'. He would forever remain a Prussian king first, second and third. Otto von Bismarck, the architect of the fledgling state and its first chancellor, was also not a nationalist. To him Germany was an extension of Prussian power and influence. He had even chosen the date for the proclamation of the German Empire to coincide with Prussia's national day. Together, king and chancellor were now trying to reign over a political construct whose more reluctant southern member states had only joined to protect fellow Germans from the perceived threat of French invasion that Bismarck had so cleverly engineered. This made for a somewhat fragile and potentially short-lived bond that the Iron Chancellor had to fight hard to maintain. He had not even dared to hold the ceremony for the proclamation of the German Reich in any of the German states. Instead, it took place at the Royal Palace of Versailles, the heart of the defeated nation France. A fitting symbol for the centrality of the notions of struggle and war to the new Germany.

On the one hand, Bismarck could work with centuries' worth of myth-making to build a nation out of the patchwork of individual states. In its first years and decades, the German Empire busied itself to build monuments to ancient legends that were supposed to give meaning and collective memory to the newly formed Germany. Wilhelm I was even declared to be the reincarnation of the medieval king Friedrich Barbarossa.

In a German version of the Arthurian legend, Barbarossa was said to be asleep under the Kyffhäuser mountains in Thuringia, destined to return one day and restore Germany to its greatness. A vast monument to this effect was erected in the 1890s. This sense of a shared mythology was added to by many great German thinkers – among them the Brothers Grimm – who had long argued that German culture, language and historical tradition form a stronger bond than local particularism. Furthermore, the irresistible economic currents of the industrial revolution that had swept through Western Europe for over a century demanded greater coordination of resources, manpower and policy if the German states did not want to fall further behind their French and British neighbours. The rising middle classes saw the immense potential of the natural resources, favourable geography and work traditions of the German-speaking lands. If only they could be unlocked through unification.

On the other hand, cultural, economic and political ties were not enough. As Bismarck himself pointed out in his famous 1862 speech, it would take war to unify the German people. That proved as accurate before 1871 as it did after. When Bismarck decided to forge a brand-new nation state in the fires of war against Denmark, Austria and France, he created a Germany whose only binding experience was conflict against external enemies. Holding the conglomerate of what had been thirty-nine individual states together under one federal government proved difficult, and cracks began to appear before the ink on the new constitution had dried. He understood that the nation had not been moulded into one smooth whole over centuries but was really closer to a mosaic, hastily glued together with the blood of its enemies. Bismarck therefore sought to perpetuate the struggle in order to preserve his new Germany.

This was a risky strategy. The Iron Chancellor was an astute politician, perhaps one of the greatest statesmen of all time, and he understood how fragile the so-called Concert of Europe was in 1871. To introduce a new major power into the very heart of it was akin to placing a child with a trumpet into the midst of a world-class symphony orchestra. He knew the newcomer had to be quiet for some time until she had learned her craft and earned the respect of the established players. Bismarck could therefore not seek external conflict again anytime soon. Instead, he focused on internal enemies against whom he could unite the majority of the German population. The new state now encompassed many ethnic minorities such as Polish, Danish and French communities, against which Bismarck could create the contrast of German citizenship. When compared to a Frenchman, Germans would see themselves as Germans rather than Bavarians or Prussians. In addition, religion seemed another useful battleground. Two-thirds of the population within the German Empire were Protestant and one third Catholic. By secularising German society, Bismarck sought to replace religion with national sentiment, thereby creating new identity references and reducing differences between Germans. Lastly, the internationalism of the socialist movement seemed a dangerous counter-current to national identity. Bismarck declared socialists enemies of the state and so could use this too to keep the struggle of all Germans against common enemies alive.

When Wilhelm II took to the throne in 1888, the tumultuous Year of the Three Emperors, he quickly clashed with Bismarck over the issue of German unity. He recognised the same problem – economic and cultural common ground would not be enough to hold the Second Reich together – but found Bismarck's solution of Germans battling each other abhorrent. Wilhelm wanted to be the Kaiser of all Germans, beloved by his subjects. If his grandfather Wilhelm I refused to be the incarnation of Friedrich Barbarossa, it would fall to him to lead his people back to greatness. Instead of looking for enemies within the Reich, he argued, Germany must fight for its place among the great nations externally. This would forge a bond of blood and iron so strong that it could never be destroyed again. The idea that Germany's external struggle for 'a place in the sun', an empire on a par with those of Britain and France, would lead to internal unity was, of course, flawed and ultimately fatal for the Second Reich. However, at 27, the hot-headed young Kaiser lacked the political acumen of the Iron Chancellor. The latter resigned from political office as a bitter and resentful man in 1890 and left Wilhelm to take the reins of an unstable nation. There had never been a Germany without Bismarck, and when the experienced and brilliant old statesman resigned, an uncertain future dawned.

Wilhelm quickly found out that the perpetual dividing factors of religion, class, geography, culture and ethnicity – to name but a few – could not just be erased by the sheer force of personality and royal charisma he undoubtedly thought he possessed. Socialists kept on striking, Catholics still looked at the Prussian king with suspicion, and Polish separatists continued to demand their own state. Perhaps they could all be convinced that Germany was everything if they had an empire of which to be proud. Wilhelm's blunderous quest for 'a place in the sun' would eventually lead the young nation into a struggle that brought it to the brink of destruction.

When the First World War broke out in 1914, Kaiser Wilhelm was initially shocked. The Balkan war he had hoped for had suddenly turned into a large-scale European conflict. Nonetheless, he still saw an opportunity to finally bring all Germans together. On 1 August 1914, he declared, 'today we are all German brothers and only German brothers'. While recent research has dispelled the myth of widespread euphoria at the outbreak of war, there was nonetheless a feeling that the 'fatherland' had to be defended. In the end, however, the First World War proved to be too much blood and iron for the young state. In November 1918 the German nation lay defeated, its crown knocked off its head, its shield and sword cracked and its spirit broken. The arch enemy France stood ready to destroy and dismantle it, arguing that nothing but further bloodshed would ever come from a state whose national identity was built on war. The Second Reich would be destroyed where it was first proclaimed – in the Hall of Mirrors at the Palace of Versailles.

But Britain and the USA saw another Germany in the smouldering ashes of the Second Reich. The seeds of democracy and economic prosperity that had been sown by Bismarck had led to the slow and tender growth of a different national vision for Germany, one that would find its identity and its place amongst the nations of the world through trade, stability and democracy. They were right, but it would take another conflict that even overshadowed the horrors of the First World War for Germany to shake off its violent and militaristic beginnings.

The German Empire was perpetually plagued by the conflicts inherent in the process of its creation. On the one hand, Bismarck acknowledged liberal traditions by introducing universal male suffrage, which allowed for the evolution of a genuinely pluralistic multi-party system, but on the other hand, this system came under constant strain from the Prussian authoritarianism at the top. The indefatigable struggle of conflicting identities that rivalled and sometimes overshadowed national identity led to Bismarck and Wilhelm II both deliberately perpetuating conflict in order to create a platform against which unity could be created. Neither established a prosperous and united state in their own times but (willingly or not) they both helped sow the seeds for the economic and democratic powerhouse Germany was to become eventually.

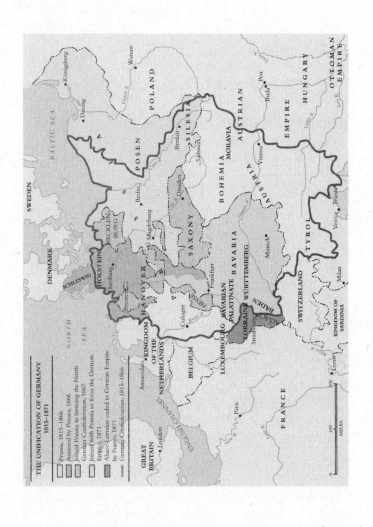

THE UNIFICATION OF GERMANY
1815–1871

Prussia, 1815–1866
Annexed by Prussia, 1866
Joined Prussia in forming the North
German Confederation, 1867
Joined with Prussia to form the German
Empire, 1871
Alsace-Lorraine ceded to German Empire
by France, 1871
German Confederation, 1815–1866

1

RISE 1815-71

'Not through speeches and majority decisions will the great questions of the day be decided ... but by iron and blood.'

Otto von Bismarck

1815: Germans Make a Stand

'To My People'* was the title of the dramatic and passionate plea of the Prussian king Friedrich Wilhelm III in 1813 to all his subjects to help liberate the German lands from French occupation. As to who his people were, even the monarch himself did not seem to be entirely sure. The first section of his appeal is addressed to 'Brandenburgers, Prussians, Silesians, Pomeranians, Lithuanians', but as his tone becomes more emotional, he switches to 'Prussians' and finally 'Germans' when he asks for the nation to rally together in the face of a 'foreign' enemy. Friedrich Wilhelm seemed conscious of the fact that his

---

* Friedrich Wilhelm III's Call for National Mobilisation, 'To My People' (17 March 1813).

subjects had layers of national identity. Strong regional loyalties stood in the way of national sentiment during peacetime but would fade into the background when Germans were pitted against a hostile external force. The almost compulsive pattern of Germany's battle for nationhood was set for the century to come.

Fittingly, the year that Napoleon was finally beaten conclusively at Waterloo was also the year Otto von Bismarck was born: 1815. His childhood, just like that of most Germans growing up at the time, was heavily coloured by stories of the struggle against the French. When Napoleon's army inflicted a humiliating defeat on Prussia in the twin battles of Jena and Auerstedt in 1806, it subjugated all Prussians to French overlordship. Even worse than the military failure in the eyes of many was the Peace of Tilsit in 1807, in which the Prussian king ceded about half of his territory and people to France, giving up all lands west of the River Elbe. This was a humiliating concession, and Friedrich Wilhelm came under immense pressure to act. He was already perceived as a meek and indecisive leader who had hesitated far too long in the face of French aggression. The contrast to his legendary Prussian forebear Friedrich the Great could not have been clearer. The 'Old Fritz' had earned his affectionate nickname in a series of successive military victories (including against France in 1757), often leading his men into battle in person, putting himself in such danger that several horses were shot from under him. By contrast, Friedrich Wilhelm's only saving grace was his beautiful and popular wife, Louise. An intelligent, strong-willed and charming woman, it was she who famously tried to stand up to Napoleon at Tilsit and negotiate better terms for Prussia. Unsuccessful as this was, it made her a figure of great public standing. But it also made her husband look even weaker. Having fled Berlin to the very edge of his realm in East Prussia, Friedrich Wilhelm had lost his battles, his capital, his dignity and the support of his people. A real low point for Prussia, it nevertheless unified many German people in their outrage. A collective sense of humiliation and shame may not be the stuff of national folklore, but it did create a defensive bond between Germans that could be called upon by future leaders.

Otto von Bismarck's parents were newlyweds when the French army occupied their home town of Schönhausen, just a few miles east of the River Elbe, behaving appallingly and plundering the village in the process. When Friedrich Wilhelm's call to arms finally came in 1813, it seemed a liberating and uplifting moment to Karl and Wilhelmine as it did for most people in the occupied German territories. No sacrifice would be too great to restore national dignity and honour. This was something worth fighting and even dying for. Ironically, it was at least in part the Prussian king's weakness that led to an ever-strengthening feeling of national resistance. When Queen Louise tragically died in 1810 at the young age of 34, she became the icon of a German patriotic movement that would pressurise successive Prussian governments to rally all Germans behind a common cause. The image of the young Louise standing up for Prussia and Germany, not afraid to confront the mighty Napoleon, provided a powerful morale boost to her grieving husband. When Napoleon's armies at last suffered a major defeat in the winter of 1812 in the Russian campaign, Friedrich Wilhelm finally found the resolve to act. His powerful speech in the spring of 1813 rallied the Prussian people behind their king and a solidifying notion of *fatherland*. Regardless of class, creed, gender, age or region, many ordinary people responded to his call. They joined voluntary army units, donated 'Gold for Iron', founded charitable clubs and societies and helped look after the wounded.

However, it was far from easy to remove Napoleon's troops from the German lands. In a series of long, drawn-out confrontations, 290,000 Germans would be called upon to fight. The spectacular climax of this was the Battle of Leipzig in October 1813 where 500,000 people fought on all sides – the largest land battle in Europe before the twentieth century. Later dubbed the Battle of the Nations, it went down in German history as a milestone on the path to nationhood. The German people, so the narrative goes, rose against their French oppressors and thus liberated themselves from the yoke of foreign dominion. As early as 1814, people were campaigning for a memorial to be built at the site of the battle, and philosophers such as Ernst Moritz Arndt amplified such demands. The monument that was eventually commissioned in 1898 would stand 299ft tall – a landmark that can be seen for miles, as imposing now as it was then. Interestingly, it was primarily funded by people's donations and the city of Leipzig rather than the federal government or the Kaiser. Over 100,000 people attended the inauguration in 1913, showing just how popular the myths and legends of Germany's creation had become.

Bismarck and his contemporaries thus grew up in a world full of stories about the heroic effort and beautiful spirit of the Wars of Liberation, as they became known. The volunteers that the Prussian king had called up in his 1813 appeal were called *Landwehr* units, and they made up 120,565 of the 290,000 men in the land army. They were further supported by various *Freikorps* units and additional volunteers from Prussia and the other German states. What made this the stuff of legend was not only the fact that these men provided such a large proportion of the fighting effort and therefore made the expulsion of the French possible. More importantly, they did not swear their oath of loyalty to Prussia like the regular army. Their allegiance lay with the German fatherland. The colours of the famous *Lützow* volunteer corps, which eventually accounted for 12.5 per cent of Prussia's fighting force, would ultimately inspire a patriotic movement with a long-lasting legacy – they wore black cloth, red trim, and gold-coloured brass buttons. The German tricolour was born.

Interestingly, the Battle of Waterloo on 18 June 1815 never reached the same central status in the German national psyche as it has done in British or French collective memory. Yes, Napoleon was defeated for good, and yes, Prussia and Austria were taken seriously at the negotiations over the future of Europe due to their contributions to the anti-French alliance. Still, German history was made at Leipzig as far as German patriots were concerned. The Battle of the Nations, in the very heart of the German lands, had far greater appeal as the climax of a heroic struggle for nationhood than a Prussian contribution to a battle fought on Dutch soil. Nonetheless, 1815 was as much of a watershed moment for Germany as it was for the rest of Europe. It was the beginning of a new balance of power and a chance for the German states to carve out a place for themselves within it.

Negotiations at the Congress of Vienna (1814–15) proved awkward and frustrating for Prussia. It felt it deserved a say in the redistribution of land and sought to acquire the Kingdom of Saxony in order to extend its domination further into central Germany. The British Foreign Minister, Lord Castlereagh, supported the Prussian plan. He wished for a unified and reliable German state to take charge of central Europe and act as a barrier to any future aggression from France. However, it was met with stiff resistance from the host of the conference, Austrian Foreign Minister Count Klemens von Metternich. Austria was still economically and politically the more mature and powerful German state. A compromise had to be found, and Saxony ended up being partitioned with Prussia receiving about 40 per cent of the territory. Interestingly, the Prussians insisted that this include the town of Wittenberg, where Martin Luther had nailed his ninety-five theses to the door of the cathedral almost 300 years earlier, kick-starting the Reformation. This piece of German history had already become a central element of the unification movement. Students and intellectuals held massive political rallies at the Wartburg where Luther hid out for 300 days after he had been declared a heretic by the Church, and crucially it was where he translated the Bible into German. He was celebrated not only for his unifying linguistic influence but also because Protestant patriots saw strong parallels between the Reformation and the Liberation Wars against the French centuries later. Germany would always throw off the yoke of foreign oppression through the sheer force and willpower of its people – be that against Napoleon or the Pope in Rome – so the narrative ran. The Prussian representatives simply could not afford to leave Vienna without the prize of Wittenberg. This was no skin off Catholic Austria's nose, and so the compromise was agreed.

The change at Vienna that had the most momentous consequences for the future formation of the German Reich was the allocation of a large block of territory along the River Rhine to Prussia. Britain wanted to ensure that there was a secure and reliable German bulwark in central Europe to keep potential French aggression at bay and to fill the power vacuum that the Habsburg retreat from Belgium had created. Austria had got tired of the thankless task of managing the vexatious Belgians and was all too happy to pass this responsibility on to Prussia. This suited all sides and was agreed upon readily. Prussian influence – more by accident than design – now spanned the entire northern half of Germany. The only fly in the ointment was that the new territories were separated from the Prussian heartlands to the east by the smaller states of Hanover, Brunswick and Hesse-Kassel. Nonetheless, it was a vast expansion of power, resources and people that would add weight to Prussian dominance in the decades to come.

The year 1815 thus marked a momentous turning point in the history of the emergent German Empire. While nationalism had existed as a strong cultural undercurrent to other developments in the German lands before the Napoleonic invasion, it took this existential foreign threat to galvanise the masses behind a common aim. The passionate support for the fatherland that was seen in the *Landwehr* and *Freikorps* units whose volunteers made a game-changing contribution to the Liberation Wars was matched by the relentless efforts of the 'Gold for Iron' campaigns and other civil movements. Thus every man, woman and child in the German territories had felt the same unnerving threat to their culture, their language and their budding nationhood, and many had made considerable sacrifices to defend this. This collective experience had tremendous psychological binding power. As historian Neil MacGregor has shown in his epic account of German cultural history, the experience of the Napoleonic Wars was matched in unifying power only by the horrors of the Thirty Years' War 200 years earlier. A spirit of defensive nationalism had taken hold that would lead to both the creation and the destruction of the German Empire.

1815–40: Two German Rivals

The Congress of Vienna was also watched with apprehension by many German nationalists who hoped that the redrawing of the European map would bring about a more unified Germany. They would be bitterly disappointed as Austria actively sought to contain a Prussian-led move towards further German unification. Prussia still acknowledged Austrian superiority and was aiming for a system that would allow both German powers to work together to control the smaller states in some form of union. For this to be possible, they argued, there needed to be a meaningful central government through which political, economic and social policy could be determined and enforced. Austria, on the other hand, feared that this would mean levelling up with Prussia, and it sought to preserve its status as the senior power. So Austrian Foreign Minister Klemens von Metternich argued for a looser confederation of German states that would be led by Austria. As both of the two leading nations at Vienna, Britain and Austria, agreed on this point, a decision was made against the Prussian model. A German Confederation, the *Deutscher Bund*, was set up.

The *Bund* as a form of German unification was hugely disappointing not only for the Prussian elites but also for many ordinary people who had just fought tooth and nail for their fatherland and wanted to see a tangible outcome for their heroic struggle. On the plus side, the *Bund* did not seek a return to the multitude of states and principalities of the Holy Roman Empire. Napoleon had needed to be able to control the German lands he had conquered and thus cajoled, threatened, bribed and beat the smaller German states into the so-called Confederation of the Rhine, which consisted of thirty-six states in 1808 and excluded only Austria, Prussia and their vassal states. The *Bund* replicated this loosely and encompassed thirty-nine German states in its finalised form. This seemed a step forward from the hundreds of administrative units of the crumbling Holy Roman Empire, but the problem was that it had almost as little centralisation of power. Its only federal organ, the *Bundesversammlung*, was in effect a regular congress of diplomats rather than a parliament with legislative power over the states. No meaningful economic, political or social coordination was possible under such a system. To add insult to injury, the chairmanship of the *Bund* was permanently given to Austria without rotation or election. Recently, historians have begun to question the idea that this constituted a loose bond as none of the states was allowed to leave it and confederation law stood above state law in principle. Both of these assertions are true, but in reality, the *Bund* never imposed federal decisions on the entirety of its member states beyond an obligation for mutual defence in case of a foreign attack. The confederation was a step towards unification when compared to the Holy Roman Empire, with the key differences being that it had a more manageable number of member states and that these states could be compelled to fight (by contrast, the Holy Roman Emperor had to rely on fragile, negotiated alliances). Ultimately, however, the *Bund* amounted to little more than a defensive agreement.

This solution caused huge frustration among the ranks of the patriotic idealists who were hoping for a more substantial answer to the German Question than that which the Austrian-led *Bund* had to offer. Their dream of a German nation state was as much out of reach as it had ever been. In the nationalist afterglow of the Liberation Wars, many vehicles for such sentiment were found. One example was the creation of *Burschenschaften*, nationalist student fraternities at German universities. The University of Jena was (and still is) the spiritual home of these societies. The *Urburschenschaft*, Germany's first such organisation, was founded there in 1815 and adopted the black-red-gold banner as their colours. These fervent young intellectuals were angry when their nationalist dreams came to nothing at Vienna, and they began to organise rallies and demonstrations that would ultimately contribute to the revolution of 1848. Events such as the *Wartburg Festival* of 1817 or the student march on Hambach Castle in 1832 provided a heady cocktail of ideas, combining the call for unification with demands for more democracy, individual rights and liberalism.

They were supported by other intellectual figures such as the philosophers Fichte and Hegel (who both had ties to Jena). Recent research has shown that their branding as 'German nationalists' is not entirely correct and must be seen in the context of later nineteenth-century sentiments. Kaiserreich scholars in the 1880s and '90s were looking for ideological founding fathers and created a somewhat simplistic reputation for both men that would last for a long time. Nonetheless, there is no denying that as influential thinkers they had a sizable impact and helped shape the direction of the liberal–nationalist movement of the first half of the nineteenth century. Nationalist writers like Ernst Moritz Arndt also became central to the unification movement. His song, '*Was ist des Deutschen Vaterland?*', practically acted as a national anthem.

On a more popular level, the Brothers Grimm played their part in the cultural unification that followed the Napoleonic Wars. Published in 1812 and 1815, their collection of German fairy tales provided nothing new in content. Stories about big bad wolves, girls locked up in towers and witches in forests had scared German-speaking children for centuries, but the Grimms' contribution lay in standardising these oral folktales into one written form. They intentionally set out to create a shared cultural good for all German speakers, unify the way they spoke, the morals they believed in and their childhood experiences, so that over generations a cultural bond would form. Obedience is a theme of many of the tales, and children often end up suffering terrible fates after they fail to listen to their elders. Little Red Riding Hood is one such example. Sending her off through the dark forest with cake and wine to see her ill grandmother, her mother had explicitly told the young girl not to stray from the path. The Grimms added this parental warning, which does not appear in Charles Perrault's French version. Of course, Little Red Riding Hood is easily tempted off the path by the false charms of the big bad wolf. As a result of this diversion, the beast is able to get to granny's house first. He devours the old lady and later, in cunning disguise, her granddaughter, too. The dangers of filial disobedience were thus vividly reinforced in every German child's mind. The forest is a recurring setting in the tales. It is always a dangerous and dark place, in contrast to the safety and tranquillity of the village. In this context, the hunter, a courageous man who dares brave such dangers, often emerges as the hero. And so a common set of imagery and morals was created. It is tempting to dismiss this as trivial, but the psychological role of shared cultural childhood experiences can hardly be underestimated. Combined with the powerful bond created by the sacrifices of the Liberation Wars, the Grimms' linguistic and cultural influence added to a growing sense of *Volk* – the idea of a German people.

Since the end of the Second World War, the word 'nationalism' has become so associated with right-wing politics that it is worth reminding ourselves that the form it took in nineteenth-century Europe was heavily coloured by liberal and romantic ideals. Like the Brothers Grimm, many believed there was beauty in national culture, identity and language. Romantic artists such as Caspar David Friedrich enjoyed immense popularity. His paintings often featured pensive figures overlooking iconic German landscapes, emphasising the almost mythical connection between people and land. His 1818 painting, *The Wanderer above the Sea of Fog*, is the best known example. It was later followed by heroic depictions of Germania, a female personification of national identity, who is usually shown strong, broad-shouldered and battle-ready. By contrast, the French Marianne tends to be painted in a more feminine form that emphasises liberty and beauty rather than defiance and bravery. Romanticism, liberalism and nationalism went hand in hand.

The conservative elites throughout Europe were still fighting to suppress the shockwaves of the French Revolution in the aftermath of the Vienna Congress. Meanwhile, German nationalists demanded a centralised state in the hope that this would allow for the setting up of a meaningful parliament while weakening the influence of arbitrary monarchical rule. They were bitterly disappointed when they saw that the major European powers had conspired to preserve the existing political order rather than reform it. But the wheels of liberalism had been set in motion and were now hard to contain. Friedrich Wilhelm had felt it necessary to make concessions to his people in the context of his appeal for volunteers in 1813, and to take these rights back now created nothing but outrage. Though still small in scale, attempted uprisings became more and more frequent throughout the 1830s. In April 1833 students even tried to disrupt a meeting of the *Bundesversammlung* in Frankfurt. This was deemed so dangerous that both Prussia and Austria sent troops to pacify the city. Despite the intense rivalry between the two German powers, they could both agree that all attempts towards radical political reform must be suppressed. Together they led a conservative backlash against the liberal ideals that took hold in the German lands, introducing censorship and tight controls over the political activity of the German people. However, this only meant that anger kept simmering under the lid of oppression until it finally boiled over in 1848.

Economically Prussia made huge gains in the lands it had been given in 1815 along the River Rhine. The Ruhr coalfield alone is one of the largest in the world, and there were further coal reserves near Aachen and in the Saar region. In addition, large amounts of iron ore could be sourced from deposits near Koblenz, and other vital resources were also in plentiful supply such as lead, zinc, copper and slate. By far the most important item was coal. As a largely agrarian nation and with central

Europe still in its industrial infancy, Austria did not foresee the powerful economic hand this acquisition dealt Prussia. The Rhineland has rightly been described as the 'richest jewel in the crown of Prussia'.*

The only problem now was that Prussia could not use the German Confederation to make the most of its new resources in the west. With its territory split down the middle, it was forced to negotiate with individual states over everything from setting up transport links to customs regulations. The resources in the Rhineland enabled and encouraged a boom in railway building. From the modest beginnings of the first line from Berlin to Potsdam in 1838, Prussia had a lot of work to do to catch up with the speed of the industrial revolution in other Western European countries, especially Britain. Economic coordination was not just desirable but essential. As help from Austria could not be expected, Prussia pressed ahead independently and set up a customs union, the *Zollverein*, in 1984. Prince Metternich was not impressed, and Austria never joined the organisation. The *Zollverein* finally made it possible to coordinate infrastructure, resources and people to develop Germany's full industrial potential. Unforeseen by the great powers at Vienna in 1815, they had given Prussia the means to unify Germany economically. By 1866 a map of the *Zollverein* looked remarkably similar to a map of the German Empire that would emerge in 1871. Historian William Carr was right to call it the 'mighty lever of German unification'.

But no matter how strong the ideological, cultural and economic amalgamation was in the 1830s, it was again the threat of a foreign enemy that rallied Germans together much more than words or money could. This enemy came in the shape of Germany's favourite adversary, France. The Second French

---

*   Chisholm, pp.242–43.

Revolution of 1830 had brought the restored Bourbon monarchy under Charles X down and installed Louis Philippe of the House of Orléans as king. While now tied to the concept of popular sovereignty, drawing his authority from the French people rather than God, the monarchy in France remained under constant challenge from republican elements who wanted to see it gone entirely. Louis Philippe's reign was therefore marked by a struggle for popularity and consent. The monarchy was further weakened when, after an unsuccessful attempt to gain influence in Egypt, the Oriental Crisis of 1840 caused France some serious political embarrassment at home and abroad. Keen to distract from this blunder, the French Prime Minister* Adolphe Thiers created conflict closer to home. He demanded that the River Rhine be reinstated as the natural border between Germany and France and called up nearly 500,000 conscripts to show that he was serious. In fairness to the French government, King Louis Philippe was not best pleased and replaced Thiers in October with the more diplomatic Francois Guizot. Meanwhile, on the other side of the Rhine, the German Confederation showed that it could act as a useful diplomatic tool and did its best to resolve the crisis peacefully. But it was too late. The bitter memories of the Napoleonic Wars and older conflicts were whipped up into a nationalist frenzy on both sides. In Germany patriotic songs were composed such as Nicholaus Becker's 'Sie sollen ihn nicht haben, den freien deutschen Rhein' (They must not get the free German Rhine); Max Schneckenburger's 'Die Wacht am Rhein' (The Watch on the Rhine) and most prolifically, Hoffmann von Fallersleben's 'Das Deutschlandlied', which is Germany's national anthem today. A continental power, wedged between Russia and France

---

*   He was also the Foreign Minister and therefore held doubly responsible for the crisis.

while lacking the security of definite and impregnable physical boundaries, Germany's national psyche was hypersensitive to the threat of invasion. The intense defensive nationalism that a foreign enemy could conjure up in German hearts and minds would never be matched by political arguments, fairy tales or economic interest.

1840–48: A German Revolution

'German history reached its turning-point and failed to turn.'* Despite his work now being over 75 years old, A.J.P. Taylor's famous judgement of the 1848 revolutions still holds water today. Uprisings and unrest swept through all of Europe as the struggle for the ideas of the French Revolution was met with stern resistance from the conservative elites. But in Germany, this took on a somewhat different form. Here was a people with a growing sense of national belonging but increasingly divided over the character of the union they sought to build. Unsuccessful as it was in bringing about meaningful immediate change, the 1848 revolution set in motion powerful and long-lasting forces that would shape German history for better and for worse.

As the nationalist euphoria of the 1840 Rhine Crisis began to subside, support for the elites who ran the German Confederation began to fade with it. The old dissatisfaction with the lack of social and political reform returned. People expected nothing less from old Prince Metternich of Austria, whose political career had now spanned three decades and was entirely dedicated to the *ancien régime*. Instead liberal and reformist hopes were pinned on Prussia. Had not Friedrich

---

* Taylor, p.71.

Wilhelm III repeatedly promised a constitution, the last time in the wake of the Vienna Congress in 1815? The demonstrations of the 1830s were trying to hold him to this promise, but when he died in 1840 after a prolonged fever and was buried next to his cherished wife Louise, many people were willing to forgive the old king and looked to his son Friedrich Wilhelm IV for change. They would be bitterly disappointed. He famously declared that 'no piece of paper will come between myself and my people'. A contract between him and his subjects would run contrary to his unshakable conviction in the Divine Right of Kings. His authority came from God, not the people.

Under other circumstances, the German people might have been forgiving towards such views, but Friedrich Wilhelm IV was the least charismatic Prussian monarch for generations. Since childhood, even his friends and family called him 'the flounder', an allusion to his podgy figure, short neck and poor posture. It quickly became apparent that this was not just a physical trait. His lack of political acumen and clumsy use of language matched his appearance. Through the 1840s he gained a reputation as a floundering, unmanly and soft fool, and this perception spanned the entire political spectrum, from enemies to supporters. His initial attempts to make peace with the reformers by relaxing censorship a little and releasing some political prisoners were seen as clumsy window dressing. It did not help that his younger brother Wilhelm, who would later become the first German Kaiser, had been put in charge of the king's cavalry and sought to make a name for himself in this position. As Friedrich Wilhelm dithered every time there was an uprising or a demonstration, his brother stepped in to quell the unrest with bloodshed. Wilhelm famously remarked, '*Gegen Demokraten helfen nur Soldaten*' – only soldiers can help against democrats. The combination of the flounder and the despot was as unpopular with radicals as it was with moderates and helped fan the flames of revolution in the 1840s.

The atmosphere of political oppression became almost unbearable for reformists. The Carlsbad Decrees, which had been introduced in all states of the German Confederation in 1819, made it legal to imprison and even execute political reformers. They were squarely aimed at the growing liberal and nationalist movements and banned patriotic fraternities, left-wing newspapers and the teaching of liberal ideas in schools and universities. This drove people such as Karl Marx into exile, but many thinkers and philosophers like him set up shop in Paris or London, where they could publish their ideas freely.

Revolution may well have remained an intellectual fantasy had it not been for the serious social problems that plagued Germany and Europe in the first half of the nineteenth century and specifically in the 1840s. Industrialisation had brought about socio-economic changes of unprecedented speed and impact. In the transformation from agrarian to industrial economy, people flocked to the cities, where overcrowding was rapidly leading to squalid living conditions, outbreaks of disease and the disruption of traditional family support networks. Fuelled by unprecedented population growth, a sizable semi-skilled underclass began to develop. Being crammed together in the city, they were more prone to politicisation than they had been in the countryside. The liberal Austrian politician Victor von Andrian-Werburg summed up the situation in his 1841 work, *Austria and its Future*: 'When has there ever been greater material misery, when has humanity ever bled from deeper and more terrible wounds than just now? Thousands of people are, in the midst of a rich, ever-growing civilisation, orphaned, forgotten and exposed to nameless misery.'[*]

---

[*] Andrian-Werburg, p.24.

Skilled workers and craftsmen were suffering too as they struggled to compete with the automation of their trades. In a move comparable to the Luddite Rebellion in England thirty years before, thousands of Silesian weavers smashed machinery in 1844 in a desperate attempt to save their livelihood and identity. Prussian state authorities responded by sending in the military, who in turn lost control and fired into the masses. On the back of the king's professed sympathy with the plight of the weavers, this seemed nothing short of callous and despotic. The incident was quickly picked up by Karl Marx, Heinrich Heine and other critics of the regime. The anger had reached a dangerous boiling point. Between 1844 and 1847 poor wheat and rye harvests and a potato blight poured oil onto the embers of misery that had already been fanned by low wages, mass unemployment and rising food prices. An anonymous pamphlet entitled 'German Hunger and the German Aristocracy' summed up the anger: 'Like a beast of the desert, a hollow-eyed and bony fellow roams the German lands and attacks his prey: Hunger. Is he after the fat cats? No, he is not like the others; this predator has a special taste: he is only after famished prey.'* Even partial censorship of such work could not quell the anger about the social injustice any longer. Revolutions broke out all over Europe in March 1848.

On 13 March 1848, relatively peaceful demonstrations were held in front of the royal palace in the heart of Berlin. Situated on an island in the River Spree, the imposing baroque building had long dominated the cityscape, but the construction of the massive dome, which had been under way since 1845, nearly doubled its height to 197ft. Following the king's own design, the cupola literally lifted this symbol of royal power

---

*   Translated from: Anonymous pamphlet 1847. www.dhm.de/lemo/bestand/objekt/nn002955

to new heights and thus served as the perfect backdrop to the demonstrations. These gatherings were primarily motivated by hunger and misery, but agitators from radical, reformist, nationalist and liberal movements had politicised the masses, and this frightened Friedrich Wilhelm IV and his brother. The former responded, as per usual, with dithering and indecision, but Prince Wilhelm chose to act and sent in the cavalry, who opened fire on the masses. Several civilians were killed. This time the anger had reached fever pitch and the masses would not be cowed again. Instead of retreating, they built street barricades and were thus able to push the fight further and further into the heart of Berlin, where the situation came to a head on 18 March. Three hundred civilians and 100 soldiers would lose their lives; around 700 people were severely injured. Fearing a further escalation of events, the floundering king gave in, and a bizarre spectacle took place. When the funeral procession for those shot in the demonstrations passed by the palace the next day, Friedrich Wilhelm stepped on to his balcony and tipped his hat in respect. Two days later, he even joined a procession of demonstrators who were marching through the streets of Berlin. Riding along on horseback and donning the German tricolour, which had hitherto been like a red rag to a bull to him, he seemed to acknowledge the anger of his subjects. Secretly, however, the king cynically accepted that his government and for that matter his life depended on this sign of goodwill. The next day, he wrote to his brother Wilhelm: 'Yesterday I had to be seen to wear the tricolour willingly in order to save everything; [...] once this trick has worked, I will take it off again!'*

In the wake of the dramatic events in Berlin, there was real excitement in the air. The king had apparently joined the movement, and now reform would take place. The German

---

★   Quoted and translated from Schwibbe, p.104.

Confederation's national assembly in Frankfurt, as well as its Prussian counterpart, were holding elections for the first time, returning parliaments dominated by liberals. They immediately began to plan for a united Germany. A constitution was drafted with plans for an all-German Kaiser at its head. The tricolour of the revolutions was to be its flag and the 'Deutschlandlied' its anthem. Hoffmann von Fallersleben's song, in particular, had considerable influence. Ironically sung to the melody of Joseph Haydn's hymn to Francis II, Emperor of the Austrian Empire, the lyrics called on Germans to value their fatherland 'above everything in the world'. Then, this phrase meant that the particularism that had stood in the way of German unity for too long should be left behind. The aggressive reinterpretation of the Nazis nearly 100 years later would make this verse unacceptable to successive German governments. The national anthem is now the third verse of the 'Deutschlandlied', beginning with the liberal values of the 1848 revolution, *'Einigkeit und Recht und Freiheit'* – unity, justice and freedom.

There was so much optimism in the air that even Karl Marx decided to return to his home country after having just published his *Communist Manifesto* in London in February. But it would all come to nought. A counter-revolution was already under way. In autumn 1848, the king first pushed the Prussian assembly out of Berlin and then dissolved it altogether. Meanwhile, the Frankfurt assembly was bitterly divided, and their last hope rested on the unity that could come from the Prussian king's leadership. They offered Friedrich Wilhelm the German crown and thereby an opportunity to finally fulfil their dreams of a united Germany under one Kaiser. Friedrich Wilhelm declined it, arguing that he could not possibly accept a crown that sprung from 'revolutionary seeds'. The local and national constitutions that had been drafted were watered down or abolished in 1849 and 1850. The national assembly in Frankfurt collapsed under its internal strife, and both the Habsburgs and Hohenzollern houses recovered their confidence and began a fierce counter-revolution to restore the old order once more. All was as it had been.

Or was it? While the last flickering embers of the revolution were snuffed out all over the German lands by the Prussian armies, a sense of German national identity had begun to emerge that could no longer be put back in the box by Austrian and Prussian traditionalists. This had been the case in Prussia for a long time, as we have seen. But the 1840s, and the 1848 revolution specifically, also saw growing nationalism in the Catholic south. It was a painful memory that Napoleon had made allies of the southern states of Bavaria, Baden and Württemberg and their troops marched side by side with the French when they entered Berlin and subjugated Prussia. The Bavarian King Ludwig was deeply troubled by the way the French had managed to weaken the German people by driving such a toxic wedge between them that they ended up fighting each other for him. So he wanted to make a statement of unity and had a monument called 'Walhalla' built. Opened in 1842, it is a memorial to Germans who have distinguished themselves. Anyone could (and can) be nominated to be commemorated there, irrespective of region, gender, class or religion. The only criterion was (and is) that candidates must be 'of the German tongue'. Even in Bavaria, perhaps the state most sceptical of Protestant Prussian overlordship, a romanticised desire for German unity was budding.

But 1848 also revealed and intensified a lot of the issues that would divide Germans and haunt their future Empire long after it was formally unified. Marx's *Communist Manifesto* may not have looked like much physically – a thin, flimsy and grey booklet that had been produced on the cheap – but the ideas in it would have profound effects on Germany, Europe and the world. Socialist and communist thought would be a powerful driver of working-class movements and an ideology to scare the elites and the middle classes into panicked over-reaction. It helped create a class consciousness that would match the existing regional, cultural and religious divisions in creating fault lines and strife. Both Bismarck and Wilhelm would fear the spectre of communism that was supposedly haunting Germany and Europe, and both sought to control it by perpetually feeding the defensive nationalism that had proved so effective through the first half of the nineteenth century.

Nonetheless, the 1848 revolution solidified the German dream. It gave a flag, an anthem and some real hope to a nationalist movement that had already grown across the German lands. Besides, by offering the German crown to Prussia and not to Austria, the Frankfurt assembly had in effect decided the future boundaries of the nation state. The long debate over *Großdeutschland* and *Kleindeutschland* (a Germany with or without Austria) had been settled. In the minds of the German people, there was now a firm national concept. Perhaps German history did not turn in 1848, but the forces of liberalism, communism and nationalism were certainly setting their wheels in motion. Vienna and Berlin would only be able to cling on to their world order for two more decades.

1850–62: The Rise of the Crazy Junker

Right from his birth in the fateful year of 1815, Otto von Bismarck's life remained remarkably intertwined with historical events. His father Karl was a *junker*, a landed Prussian aristocrat, from an old family that had held the Schönhausen estate for centuries. His mother Wilhelmine was the daughter of a cabinet secretary. From his parents he inherited a peculiar mix of ultraconservative instincts and exceptional political cunning. The second son of a moderately successful but not particularly distinguished couple, young Otto spent most of his early years uncertain about his future and his place in the world. Throughout the 1830s and early 1840s, he led the life of a drifter. He drank heavily, had numerous affairs and gambled, accumulating huge debts during his time at university, apparently enjoying himself immensely in the process. He later bragged that he had been in twenty-eight sword fights in his first three semesters alone. Having tried his hand at careers in law, the civil service and the military, he decided to return to his father's estate in 1839. Managing affairs in rural Pomerania, however, brought him little joy or satisfaction. The years from 1839 to 1847 went by marked by boredom, frustration and loneliness. Bismarck tried to make up for this with an excessive lifestyle of drinking, hunting and womanising, so much so that he became known as 'the crazy *junker*' in the local area. Writing to a student friend in 1845, he complained: 'My only company consists of dogs, horses and country junkers, and I enjoy some regard in the eyes of the latter because I can read writing easily [and] dress like a human being at all times [...] I smoke terribly strong cigars and drink my guests under the table with friendly efficiency.'* His personal life finally stabilised in 1847 when he married the kind and modest Johanna von Puttkammer, who would be a lifelong companion and rock of stability to him. Just in time to get involved in the political excitement of the 1848 revolution.

When Bismarck decided to take up a seat in the Prussian parliament called by Friedrich Wilhelm in 1847, he only did so because he had been asked to step in for another member who could not attend due to illness. He was utterly enthralled by the experience, enjoying the intrigue, plotting and oratory battles that came with political life. In a letter to a friend

---

*   English translation from Ullrich, *Bismarck*, p.20.

he confessed that politics had him 'in an uninterrupted state of excitement that barely allows me to eat or sleep'.* Crafting his speeches with exceptional linguistic flair while maintaining an uncompromising, ultra-conservative stance, he quickly made a name for himself as a gifted and ruthless politician. He proved this to be quite correct when, panicked by the barricade wars in Berlin in March 1848, he armed a group of peasants with shotguns to help Friedrich Wilhelm, whom he believed to be in great danger. When it looked like the king had changed sides and rode out with the protestors, Bismarck swiftly turned against him and approached his sister-in-law, Augusta, to ask if she would support a coup d'état that would put her husband, Prince Wilhelm, on the throne. Augusta never forgave him for this. She would despise him as a disloyal, scheming politician for the rest of her life, even when she became Queen of Prussia and Empress of Germany.

During the aftermath of the 1848 revolution, Bismarck busied himself to help restore royal authority. He lobbied, helped set up an influential conservative newspaper, later called the *Kreuzzeitung*, and built his reputation as a man who could persuade people to act. He got elected into the Prussian parliament once more in 1849 and supported the king whole-heartedly when he turned down the German crown. Grateful for the effective string-pulling behind the scenes, Friedrich Wilhelm gave Bismarck the immensely powerful position of Prussian envoy to the parliament of the German Confederation in Frankfurt in 1851. He had effectively become the voice of Prussia.

Bismarck used this position to isolate Prussia's rival, Austria. He frequently clashed with his Austrian counterpart Count Friedrich von Thun, whose presupposition that Prussia was the

---

*   Ibid., p.27.

junior partner when it came to controlling the German states began to irritate him. Things came to a head when Austria demanded access to the Prussian-led *Zollverein* market. Thun nonchalantly admitted that this would shift economic dominance southward but added that this was only the natural order of things. Bismarck told him in no uncertain terms that the time for Prussia had come and that he had no intention to shackle 'our trim and seaworthy frigate to the worm-eaten old battleship of Austria'.* He then added insult to injury by challenging the convention that only the Chair of the *Bund*, i.e. Friedrich von Thun, smoked during the sessions in Frankfurt. One day, in the middle of a drawn-out clash with Thun about petty protocol matters, Bismarck nonchalantly pulled a cigar out of his pocket. Provocatively, he strutted across the floor to the Chair of the German Confederation and asked him for a match. This diplomatic affront caused outrage and amusement in equal measure, no doubt much to the quarrelsome *junker*'s delight. Some newspapers reported that even non-smoking members were taking up the habit in parliament in an attempt to copy the defiant spirit of the gesture. In another episode of Bismarck's aggressive style, an argument between him and his old adversary Georg von Vincke spiralled out of control in the Prussian parliament. On 23 March 1852, Vincke was playing to the gallery when he jeered in a parliamentary session that 'all I know of [Bismarck's] diplomatic achievements is limited to the famous burning cigarette'.† When the collective heckles and whoops of the men in the room finally faded into an expectant hush, Bismarck did not even get up from his chair as he coolly retorted that Vincke's parents had apparently failed to teach him any manners. Vincke lost it and challenged Bismarck to a

---

*   Quoted from Ullrich, p.39.
†   Translated from Reichling.

life-or-death duel. Both men wrote their testaments, neither
told close family. Vincke even stated where he wanted to be
buried, wrote a tearful letter to his wife and instructed a friend
to give it to her and tell her 'gently' of his demise. Bismarck's
wife, Johanna, was pregnant and so Bismarck asked his brother-
in-law Arnim-Kröchlendorff to look after her and the baby
should the worst come to pass. On the morning of 25 March,
the two duellists, a doctor and a handful of witnesses met at
dawn on a meadow in Tegel, on the outskirts of Berlin. Ludwig
von Bodelschwingh, a man trusted by both combatants, was
supposed to act as umpire. Nervously, he asked if the matter
could not be settled peacefully. Apparently Vincke was open to
the idea but Bismarck was enjoying himself far too much. The
only concession the latter gave was to reduce the number of
shots to one, down from the original four. The duellists slowly
walked the agreed fifteen steps away from each other, turned
and fired. Both missed their mark. At this, Bodelschwingh burst
into tears and asked the rivals to shake hands and settle the
matter there and then. Although neither of the two men was
injured, the incident added to Bismarck's notoriety.

When the Crimean War erupted in 1853, it severely dis-
turbed the fragile harmony of the Concert of Europe. With the
Ottoman Empire crumbling, vast swathes of Eastern Europe
and the Middle East seemed up for grabs. Russian advances into
this power vacuum were fiercely contested by France, Britain
and the remnants of the Ottoman Empire itself. It was time
for Prussia to make a decision. In the so-called Punctation of
Olmütz, Prussia had agreed to a humiliating treaty of sub-
ordination to Austria in 1850, abandoning all plans of a
Kleindeutschland solution to the German question. Instead, it had
accepted the German Confederation as the means to make pan-
German policy. As the *Bund* was first and foremost a defensive
agreement and also still under permanent Austrian leadership,

Austria demanded the mobilisation of 150,000 men from the other thirty-eight states to support the western alliance and threaten Russia. Prussia and most of the smaller German states saw no immediate benefit to getting involved in a war from which they did not stand to gain anything. The Austro-Prussian power struggle was now out in the open, and as the Prussian envoy to the *Bund*, Bismarck sat right at the centre of events. He smoothly brushed the Austrian request for mobilisation aside and thereby gave the smaller states the confidence to do the same. It is worth pointing out that this was in no way designed to instigate collusion of the German states against Austria to work towards unifying Germany under Prussian leadership. To the contrary, Bismarck's argument ran along the lines that as the Prussian envoy to the *Bund*, he could only speak for Prussia's interest. He would not drag his kingdom into a conflict that would not benefit it. As most smaller states felt the same, they followed suit. Austria stood alone and isolated; the two German powers had drifted further apart.

When Friedrich Wilhelm IV suffered a bad stroke in 1857, his brother Prince Wilhelm took over as regent. Wilhelm had already shown that he was made of sterner stuff, but he also showed more political aptitude. The tides had changed in the aftermath of 1848, and liberalism was on the rise. No longer seen as the extremist fantasy of university students and radical intellectuals, it had become a political ideology that was increasingly acceptable even in the salons of the elites. Max von Forckenbeck was one such fashionable liberal. From a traditional aristocratic family, he became the founder of the left-liberal Progress Party in 1861. Yet he retained so much public respect even among the Prussian elites that he was later appointed Mayor of Berlin, overseeing the emergence of the German capital in the 1870s. The Prussian parliament had returned a robust liberal majority in recent elections despite the introduction of a three-tier voting system in 1848 that favoured the upper classes. Wilhelm acknowledged that times were changing and the spectre of 1848 was still looming large – he needed to work with the liberals in order to preserve Prussian and royal power. An additional problem for Wilhelm was that his son Friedrich had shown support for liberalism and thus made for a potential figurehead of future rebellions. Only 16 years old when the 1848 revolution had hit Berlin, it made a lasting impression on the young man. In 1858, he married Queen Victoria's eldest daughter, also called Victoria, much to the delight of her father Prince Albert, who had been a strong supporter of the liberal ideals of 1848. Here was a young power couple ready to democratise Prussia and unify Germany under a liberal banner when the time came. Prince Wilhelm had to act before this crystallised as a realistic option. He proclaimed his willingness to work with the movement and when he officially became King of Prussia after his brother's death on 2 January 1861, the so-called 'New Era' of Hohenzollern politics was supposedly ushered in.

Ever pragmatic, Bismarck realised that he would have to follow on this course if he wanted to further his political ambitions and become Minister President of Prussia. He sent the king a lengthy memorandum, so long in fact that it was called 'the little book', in which he argued for an extension of Prussian power into a German union. But to no avail. Bismarck's reputation as an arch-conservative bulldog of a *junker* meant that Wilhelm could not be seen to rely on him politically all the while that he had to convince the liberals that he was now a serious vehicle for their cause. So Bismarck was banished first to St Petersburg and then to Paris as Prussian envoy, between 1859 and 1862. Both were crucial posts, given the power of Russia and France. Still, they were far away from Berlin where Wilhelm was battling it out with the liberals.

The biggest issue of the day was the question over the Prussian military. Wilhelm and his inner circle were concerned by its scale and structure. Prussia's population had grown from 11 to 18 million since 1815, but the size of its land army remained at a constant 150,000. Meanwhile, France had twice that, and Russia's military was seven times as large.* This made it tricky for Prussia to build up any diplomatic weight in Europe. In addition, the voluntary *Landwehr* units that had played such a crucial role in the liberation wars against Napoleon were still part of the Prussian army. Almost by definition, those young men who decided to join the ranks of the volunteer corps did so out of a sense of idealism, to step into the footsteps of those patriots who had rallied to the defence of the fatherland in 1813. This meant that most of them were liberal nationalists whose loyalties did not lie with Prussia and its king but with the Germany they fought to establish. Therefore it is understandable that Wilhelm and his advisors felt somewhat uneasy about the idea of having an undersized army with a large contingent of members whose loyalty could not necessarily be depended upon. If there was another 1848, would they rally to defend the Prussian crown they wished to see moulded into a German one? Would they shoot on fellow members of the fraternities and societies they themselves belonged to so as to preserve the old order? Wilhelm wanted to be sure of his military. So a plan for reform was established with War Minister Count Albrecht von Roon, who had been appointed in 1859. The army would be gradually increased in size, military service would be extended to three years, and most importantly, the *Landwehr* would be abolished. This would result in a very sizable and loyal force that would provide a powerful tool for domestic and foreign policy.

---

*   Epkenhans, p.67.

The liberal-dominated Prussian parliament was outraged, and after drawn-out battles of words, it became apparent that Roon would not be able to bully or cajole members into accepting the reforms. After the 1848 bloodbath, they feared the restructuring of the army was merely intended to create a tool of oppression. Wilhelm may have given the impression that a 'new era' had begun but so did his brother in March 1848, only to plot the counter-revolution as he paraded the tricolour through the capital. The liberals had become confident, and they stood up to Roon, voting the military budget down in 1862. Wilhelm suffered a nervous breakdown and considered abdicating and leaving everything to his liberal son, Friedrich. Now it was Roon's turn to panic. The general immediately sent a telegram to Bismarck in Paris on 18 September 1862. It famously read, '*Periculum in mora. Dépêchez-vous!*' – There is danger in delay. Hurry!

What happened next foreshadowed the future relationship between Wilhelm and Bismarck. The latter immediately rushed back to Berlin – both out of a sense of duty but also because he knew his hour had finally come. In a long conversation with the king, he played cleverly to all his insecurities, his pride and his emotions. He had always had a natural talent for the use of language but had honed this further in his years as a diplomat in Frankfurt, St Petersburg and Paris. This was Bismarck in his element. With tears in his eyes, he appealed to the king that this was a matter of principle. If he gave the Prussian crown to his son, he surrendered it also to liberalism, parliamentarianism and nationalism. He would not only betray the divine right of kings but Prussia itself. Crown Prince Friedrich and those who surrounded him at home and abroad all wanted to melt down the Prussian crown in order to forge a German one. It must not come to that. Now moved to tears himself, Wilhelm asked Bismarck if he would help him save Prussia and the latter pledged his unquestionable loyalty. On 23 September 1862, Otto von Bismarck became the Minister President of Prussia. Wilhelm was utterly dependent on him.

1862–67: Blood and Iron

When Ludwig von Rochau coined the term 'realpolitik', he was trying to provide a workable strategy for the liberal–nationalist movement in the German states. He had engaged in the unsuccessful Frankfurter Wachensturm in 1833, an uprising organised by fraternities that sought to overwhelm the police, take control of the treasury of the German Confederation and thus kick-start a revolution. Consisting of only fifty students, the attacking forces were quickly overwhelmed by police and military. Rochau himself fled to France, where he spent ten years in exile. The lessons he drew from this experience and the failed revolution of 1848 were written up in his 1853 book, *Grundsätze der Realpolitik* – The Principles of Practical Politics. He argued that progressive change could not be achieved through idealistic thinking or violent action. Pragmatism was the way forward. Irrespective of the moral rights and wrongs of the means, one has to do what it takes to get as close to one's aims as possible. In the case of liberalism and nationalism in Germany, he advised working with the elites, however unpalatable this might be. He argued revolutions and high moral principle would never lead to actual change, and a more realistic and pragmatic approach was the way forward. It is then not without irony that the arch-conservative Bismarck, who fought tooth and nail against liberalism, would go down in history as the archetype of a realpolitiker.

Once appointed as Minister President of Prussia, Bismarck immediately began to tackle the conflict with parliament over the military reforms that had driven Wilhelm to the brink of despair just a few days earlier. It was in this context that Bismarck delivered his famous Blood and Iron Speech on 30 September 1862. Announcing that even without parliamentary approval he would go ahead with the planned military reforms, including an increase of the number of peacetime troops from 150,000 men to 220,000, he argued:

> Germany is not looking to Prussia's liberalism, but to its power; Bavaria, Württemberg, Baden may indulge liberalism, and yet no one will assign them Prussia's role [...] it is not by speeches and majority resolutions that the great questions of the time are decided – that was the big mistake of 1848 and 1849 – but by iron and blood.*

Essentially Bismarck justified his breaking of constitutional rules by arguing that it was the right thing to do. He saw liberalism as fanciful intellectual indulgence. It was not ideas and words that would get things done, but actions. The response to those famous words was an outpouring of anger in the liberal press, but it was like water off a duck's back to the confident Minister President. Bismarck dug his heels in over the matter and ruled without parliamentary budget approval until 1866. Parliament finally caved in and passed a Bill of Indemnity that legitimised the military spending retrospectively. Bismarck's only concession to the liberals was a promise not to do it again. He would respect the Prussian constitution and parliament's right to approve budgets. What would have been a given to most politicians, indeed even to the king himself, namely the fact that the

---

*   *Otto von Bismarck, Reden 1847–1869* (Speeches, 1847–1869), ed., Wilhelm Schüßler, vol. 10, *Bismarck: Die gesammelten Werke* (Bismarck: Collected Works), ed. Hermann von Petersdorff. Berlin: Otto Stolberg, 1924–35, pp.139–40. Translation: Jeremiah Riemer.

constitution was the fundamental law everyone had to abide by, cleverly turned into a bargaining chip in Bismarck's hands.

Another trademark of Bismarck's complete lack of political morality was his ability to make friends with his enemies when it suited him. Recognising the fact that liberals and socialists fought side by side in 1848 but for very different reasons, he set out to keep both movements separated. He met Ferdinand Lasalle, a key figure in the early establishment of the Social Democratic movement, on several occasions and held long informal talks with him. As a socialist and democrat, his views and aims could not have been further removed from Bismarck's, but the latter applied all his charm and kept Lasalle engaged in talks. Though officially kept a secret on both sides – neither man could admit to his respective political circles that he had fraternised with the class enemy – rumours spread quickly. They deeply frightened the liberals, who believed that they had been deprived of a potential ally in the fight for progressive change. This charade created a sense of defeatism and isolation in both the Progress Party Liberals under Forckenbeck and the National Liberals, now led by Bismarck's old adversary Vincke. It made them more susceptible to accepting Bismarck's political deals. This was realpolitik in action.

Bismarck applied similarly amoral tactics in his foreign policy. From October 1862, he held both the offices of Minister President and Foreign Minister. He had already made a strong impression during his time as the Prussian envoy to Russia and France between 1859 and 1862. In Paris, he became acquainted with Napoleon III, Emperor of France since 1852, and the pair got on well. Bismarck had also met Benjamin Disraeli in London in 1862 (then leader of the opposition), to whom he apparently talked openly about an inevitable war between Austria and Prussia for German supremacy. Disraeli later warned the Austrian envoy, 'be careful about that man, he

means what he says'.* Russia too would have to be convinced
to take Prussia seriously and stay on friendly terms with it. This
was partially why Bismarck had been so opposed to supporting Austria in the Crimean War. Alienating Russia would not
aid the cause of Prussian expansion in central Europe. All the
great European powers had to be convinced that here was an
ally growing stronger, not an enemy becoming over-powerful.
Without hesitation, Bismarck gave Prussia's implicit support to
the brutal crushing of the so-called January Uprising in Poland
in 1863 by Russian troops. In the Alvensleben Convention of
February 1863, both states agreed to coordinate efforts to suppress Polish nationalism, even though the risings happened on
the Russian side of the border and were dealt with entirely by
the Russian army. Nonetheless, Bismarck thereby sanctioned
the killing of thousands in battle as well as 128 political execu-
tions and the deportations of roughly 10,000 men, women and
children to Siberia. Once again, parliament was outraged and
appealed to the king. Bismarck simply nullified the agreement
with Russia a few months later, letting parliament win, but by
then the uprising had been crushed and a grateful Russia was on
good terms with the Prussian cabinet. Britain too had signified
that it was not unreceptive to an expansion of Prussian interest
so long as the Concert of Europe continued to play a harmoni-
ous tune. Thus, when later in the year Austria tried to regain
some ground through a reform of the German Confederation
in its favour, Bismarck found it easy to prevent this. To the other
thirty-seven states, it now made sense to follow Prussia's lead, an
aspiring German power with a shiny new military and robust
European support.

German and European backing secured, the time was now
ripe to expand Prussian power in territorial terms. The Danish

---

*   Weintraub, p.395.

king, Christian IX, played right into Bismarck's hands when on 18 November 1863 he decided to sign a document that practically annexed the territory of Schleswig to Denmark. The status of Schleswig and Holstein, the two duchies to the far north of the German lands, had long been the point of bitter disputes. Holstein had a mostly German-speaking population and became part of the *Bund* in 1815. Schleswig, by contrast, had a sizable Danish minority and was ruled over in a personal union with the Danish royal family while remaining outside the *Bund*. The great powers had all agreed to this compromise at the Vienna Congress in 1815, and so there was widespread concern at Christian's actions in 1863. Bismarck's initial response was to appeal to the *Bund* in Frankfurt as the federal defence mechanism to send troops to Holstein. They agreed and sent a combined force of confederation soldiers from Saxony and Hanover, the states closest to Holstein, to protect it as well as to send a clear signal to Denmark. Meanwhile, Prussia and Austria conspired to seize Schleswig in order to force the Danish king to renounce his claim over it. They formally requested permission to do so from the *Bund*. However, unlike Holstein, Schleswig was not part of the German Confederation. An occupation, for whatever reason, was akin to invasion and there was no telling how the European powers would react. Remarkably the *Bund* stood up to its two overlords and denied the request. Bavaria and Saxony even went as far as to deny Austria the right to transport goods and troops through their states. There was also talk that the Confederation army in Holstein would fight Prussian and Austrian soldiers should any be sent to Schleswig. Bismarck was not cowed. He called the bluff, and Prussian and Austrian forces crossed the River Eider from Holstein into Schleswig on 1 February 1864.

Seeing Austria and Prussia marching side by side provided a popular image that raised renewed hopes for the *Großdeutschland* solution, a greater Germany that included both Austria and Prussia. Both armies wore white armbands to signify their alliance and to revive the camaraderie of the much-romanticised Liberation Wars of 1813–15. The victory over Denmark was swift, and army painters such as Wilhelm Camphausen did their best to glorify the campaign in their work. (His *Die Erstürmung der Insel Alsen durch die Preußen 1864 – The Attack on the Isle of Also by the Prussians 1864* – was released in 1866 and showed a heroic Prussian army overwhelming a cowering group of Danes.) In the peace agreed at Vienna on 30 October 1864, Denmark had to renounce any claims over Schleswig and Holstein. Both were placed under joint Prussian and Austrian control until the Gasteiner Convention of 1865 between the two German powers led to the allocation of Schleswig to Prussia and Holstein to Austria. Despite hopes of a peaceful solution to the toxic German dualism of the previous decades, the pan-German harmony would not last long. A year later the so-called German War broke out, and Prussia and Austria battled for German hegemony.

In the spring of 1866, both German powers sought to hem the other in by making secret alliances and assurance treaties with foreign powers. Unfortunately for Austria, Bismarck had already made powerful friends in Britain, France, Russia and Italy and was therefore confident that he could prevail in a showdown with Austria. The opportunity to put that to the test came when Austria suggested that the German Confederation in Frankfurt took another look at the settlement of the Schleswig-Holstein question. Bismarck immediately cried foul play and sent Prussian troops into Austrian-occupied Holstein on 7 June 1866. Using its domination in the *Bund*, Austria called on the support of the larger states of Bavaria, Württemberg, Hanover, Saxony, Baden, Hesse, Nassau, Saxony-Meiningen, Liechtenstein, Reuß and Frankfurt. Most of the smaller northern and central states sided with Prussia. Crucially, Bismarck had also secured Italian support in April 1866.

The German War was decided after only a few weeks at the Battle of Königgrätz on 3 July 1866. In the aftermath, the Peace of Prague left Austria itself largely intact (it had to cede the region of Veneto to Italy so as to reward Italian assistance to Prussia); but it had far-reaching consequences for Prussia and the formation of a future German state. Ruthlessly annexing the larger middle states of Hanover, Hesse, Nassau and Frankfurt, Prussia finally closed the gap between its eastern and western territories and now presided over a vast European landmass from the River Memel in the east to the Rhine in the west. Prussia also declared the German Confederation null and void, ending Austrian hegemony over the German lands once and for all.

Formed as a military alliance in 1866, the North German Confederation was to be Prussia's vehicle for the expansion of its power into the newly annexed states. The twenty-two members all sat north of the River Main. Bismarck offered the southern states an opportunity to found their own South German Confederation in the hope that this would isolate Austria even further. This came to nothing as Württemberg and Baden felt they would be subjugated to Bavarian overlordship. Meanwhile, elections were held in the North German Confederation in February 1867, and the resulting parliament drafted a constitution for all member states that was ratified in April by 230 to 53 votes. Naturally, Otto von Bismarck became its chancellor on 16 July. The entire set-up was meant to be a provisional solution as Bismarck was waiting to see how the southern states would react and if France would object to the formation of what amounted to a federal North German state. Nonetheless, the end result looked suspiciously like a nation state. A new flag was ratified – a black, white and red tricolour that combined the red and white colours of the historic North German Hanseatic League with Prussia's black and white. The *Zollverein* was restructured into a relatively unified economic system, and defensive alliances were made with the southern states. Bismarck gave assurances to Napoleon III that he was merely rebuilding a loose federal agreement between the lands north of the Main. But despite this, a solid political union with economic and defensive links that put a *Kleindeutschland* solution within reach emerged from the German War. It just needed one more of Bismarck's ruthless schemes to deal with French opposition and south German reluctance in one fell swoop.

1868–71: An Empire is Born

As late as 1868, Bismarck could still not see the unification of Germany as a possibility for the near future. French apprehension was intense after the decisive outcome of the Austro-Prussian 'Brothers' War' of 1866, and the southern German states were still reluctant to forge a bond with the North German Confederation that went beyond economic and military agreements. In conversation with General-Quartermaster Suckow of Württemberg, Bismarck admitted, 'If Germany achieves its national aim in the nineteenth century, that seems to me a great thing.'* So Bismarck spent the years from 1866 to 1869 consolidating the North German Confederation and anchoring the new power block in the centre of Europe. He published the secret defensive agreements he had made with the southern German states in 1867. In doing so, he sent a powerful signal to Austria and France by indicating that they would meet an

---

*   Quoted from Ullrich, p.71.

all-German force should the aggressive Prussian annexations of 1866 be challenged.

Internally Bismarck and the North German parliament busied themselves building up an economic and political power-house that would hopefully in time be too attractive for Baden, Württemberg and Bavaria to resist any longer. The constitution, mainly Bismarck's work, incorporated the ideas of 1848 by granting universal male suffrage and freedom of movement between the member states. It also regulated trade, introduced a criminal code and standardised weights and measurements. Previously, regional differences had often led to confusion and disagreements. A Bavarian cloth merchant on the lookout for interesting wares from Brunswick, for example, would have been in for a nasty surprise or at the very least a feat of arithmetic. If he bought an 'Ell' worth of cloth there, he would be sent 57cm of the stuff, while the same measurement referred to 83cm at home. The unified legislation, combined with the vast natural resources it held, readied the North German Confederation to become a modern European power. Under these circumstances, Bismarck was not in any rush to unify Germany immediately. He knew the southern states could not be forced into a union against their will; after all, defensive nationalist sentiment had been the only vehicle for pan-German cooperation in his life-time. An external enemy was needed to forge a German crown in the fires of war, and Bismarck did not have to look far to find one.

What Bismarck needed was a conflict in which Prussia could appear as the injured party. In 1869, the perfect oppor-tunity presented itself from an unexpected source. The Spanish queen, Isabella II, had been toppled a year earlier, and a suit-able replacement had not been found. Prince Leopold of the Hohenzollern dynasty came into consideration as he was mar-ried to the Portuguese Infanta, Antónia. Needless to say that the idea of a Hohenzollern on the Spanish throne was anathema to the French, who would then be encircled by Prussian-controlled lands. Bismarck knew they would not accept it. When in the summer of 1870, the vacant Spanish throne was officially offered to the Hohenzollern prince, the chance had to be grasped. The dithering Leopold was in no way reassured by the fact that both Wilhelm I and even his own father Karl Anton von Hohenzollern were cautious about accepting the offer. Napoleon III had made it abundantly clear that he would not accept an extension of Prussian and Hohenzollern power into Spain. He said both publicly and in private that he would take this as a breach of the European balance of power and as a personal insult to the dignity of France. In other words, a Hohenzollern claim to the Spanish throne would mean war. But that was precisely what Bismarck wanted. A seemingly unprovoked attack on Prussia by France would trigger the defensive agreements between the North German Confederation and the southern states. It might, therefore, serve to melt Germany into a Prussian-dominated conglomerate. Thus poor Leopold ended up being the pawn in a game of political chess between Napoleon and Bismarck.

A few diplomatic strings were pulled in Madrid, and suddenly, on 19 June, Leopold accepted the candidacy officially. Bismarck needed to be seen to have nothing to do with this and retreated to his secluded rural estate of Varzin (which he had bought from the 400,000 Thalers he had received from Wilhelm as a reward for provoking and winning the conflict with Austria). It is a somewhat amusing notion to think of the cunning *junker* sitting back to wait for his plan to unfold from an armchair at Varzin. Still, the consequences of his war games were grave and far-reaching. When the Hohenzollern candidacy was leaked to the press and released on 2 July, earlier than planned, the news reached the French public entirely out of the blue. Reacting in the heat of the moment and giving in to injured pride, the French government walked right into Bismarck's trap. They declared the affair an affront to French dignity and would not accept an offer made by Leopold's father to withdraw the candidacy. Bismarck was delighted, the tinderbox was set up and it only needed a tiny spark to explode.

Bismarck himself provided this spark in one of his most infamous schemes, the so-called 'Ems Telegram'. The French asked Wilhelm I not only to withdraw Leopold's candidacy but also renounce any Hohenzollern claims to the Spanish throne for all time and publicly declare that he had not meant to injure French pride. This went much further than was usual by the standards of European diplomacy. Even a calm Wilhelm with little interest in the matter could not accept such demands and grovel in public before the French throne. Politely he turned down the request and asked Bismarck to phrase the telegram to the French in such a way that it would appease them without making Prussia look weak. Bismarck knew how to do these things. And he did. The problem was that he had engineered the entire situation in order to provoke war, and now the moment had come to snap the trap. He sharpened the wording of the telegram and made it look as if Wilhelm had flippantly dismissed the French ambassador Benedetti out of hand when the latter had visited the Prussian king in Bad Ems with his demands. Judging rightly that French tempers had already been frayed, he now provided the final insult. To be on the safe side and ensure that cooler heads in the government would not prevail, he leaked the wording of the explosive telegram to the press. Napoleon III and his cabinet had played their part in Bismarck's schemes perfectly, and now they were cornered. An angry French public was calling on their emperor to act; Napoleon III had no choice but to declare war on 19 July 1870.

In the eyes of the public, Prussia was clearly the injured party. Europe had looked on as French vitriol became more and more emotionally charged while the chancellor of the North German Confederation innocently holidayed on his rural estate and the king relaxed in Bad Ems. There would be no help for France from any of the European powers, and in the southern German states there was an outpouring of sympathy for Prussia. The heated passions of defensive nationalism had been kindled once more and the military agreement with the states south of the River Main was honoured. The resulting all-German force was too much for an outnumbered and underprepared French army. The decisive battle came at Sedan on 2 September 1870, where Napoleon III himself was captured. While a brave French resistance force held out a while longer, the near-constant bombardment of Paris from December 1870 proved to be the final blow.

After Sedan and successive military victories from September 1870, an intoxicating wave of nationalist sentiment swept through the German lands. Bismarck used this temporary goodwill to bring the leaders of the states together for negotiations about a federal German nation state. In November, the southern German states joined the North German Confederation, and it was agreed that the new union should be renamed as the German Empire (*Deutsches Reich*). Wilhelm himself was still hesitant. He was as reluctant to give up his beloved crown as the Bavarian King Ludwig was to give up his. Once again, Bismarck intervened. Secretly bribing Ludwig so that he would remain silent, he drafted a letter to Wilhelm, offering him the German crown, and pretended it had come from Ludwig. Even so, Wilhelm was reluctant, and it took further negotiations for him to accept the German crown formally. He insisted on the title 'Kaiser Wilhelm' rather than 'German Kaiser' as per Bismarck's plans – a sign of just how uneasy he was with the idea of merging Prussia into Germany.

The new nation state would become effective from 1 January 1871, but a more symbolic date was needed for the official proclamation. The nearest suitable anniversary was 18 January. On that very day in 1701, Friedrich III of Brandenburg had been declared Friedrich I of Prussia, uniting divided territories into one stronger whole. The carefully crafted national narrative was compelling in the warm afterglow of victory against the arch-enemy France. The German Empire was proclaimed at the Palace of Versailles to wild jubilation all across the German lands.

2

BISMARCK'S REICH
1871-88

'Laws are like sausages – it's best not to see them being made.'

Otto von Bismarck

A Brand New Empire:
Proclamation and Constitution

In contrast to the impression we get from Anton von Werner's paintings of the occasion, the proclamation of the German Empire on 18 January 1871 was a rather short and straight-forward affair. The Hall of Mirrors was a spectacular venue. Given its 73m (240ft) length, it is one of the largest rooms at the Palace of Versailles, but unfortunately, it is also a rather narrow room at 10.5m (34.4ft) width. Soldiers from the North German Confederation and the southern German states were crammed in on the window side while their officers stood opposite, in front of the mirrors. This left a narrow corridor for Wilhelm and the German princes to walk through as they entered the hall through the high doors at the end. The painter Werner was present and watched on as the German Kaiser and

The third version of *Proclamation of the German Empire in Versailles* by Anton von Werner, produced in 1885 for Bismarck's 70th birthday.

his entourage made their way to a small altar that had been erected in the centre of the hall. A short service was held. Then the group walked on to the end of the room where a platform had been set up. Kaiser Wilhelm positioned himself in the middle and was flanked by the other German princes. Bismarck proceeded to read the proclamation of the German Empire in a sober and monotonous drone. At the end, the Grand Duke of Baden exclaimed: 'Long live His Majesty Kaiser Wilhelm!' (His raised hand can be seen right behind Wilhelm in Werner's painting. Baden appears in this role in all of the painting's versions as it was the Grand Duke who introduced the painter to the Hohenzollerns in the first place. Werner was also on great terms with Friedrich, the Crown Prince.) The officers and soldiers shouted 'hurrah' in response. As the latter stood by the open windows, the assembled troops in the court-yard quickly picked up the cheers, and waves of noise swept through the crowds.

The entire set-up revealed much about the nature of the newly founded German Empire. It seems an odd choice to hold the official proclamation of a new nation on foreign soil. However, Bismarck knew that any location in the German lands would have risked raising one state above the others, compromising the fragile moment of unity. The only thing that had tied the four states south of the River Main to the North German Confederation was the threat of another 'Napoleonic' occupation. The national jubilation that came from the glorious and swift victory over France had to be upheld. Thus even the unification ceremony itself was intended to remind the German princes why they had offered Wilhelm the Kaiser crown. The magnificent ceiling of the Hall of Mirrors, with its glorification of Louis XIV as the conqueror of German lands, provided the perfect backdrop for a ceremony that celebrated the reversal of fortunes between Germany and France. Furthermore, the proclamation was set up and portrayed as an exclusively military ceremony. Bismarck, the Kaiser and the princes all appeared in uniform and celebrated the foundation of a nation state with soldiers and officers – not a civilian in sight. This was a far cry from the democratic unification of which the liberals had dreamed. At Versailles, there were no reminders of 1848 – no tricolour, no 'Deutschlandlied'. Just marching bands and formalities in the heart of a humiliated enemy. Bismarck was right; the German Empire had not been made with speeches and majority decisions; it had been forged in blood and iron.

The German Empire was a formidable force in Europe right from the outset. It held 41 million people and thus became the largest Western European nation overnight. France (36 million),

Britain (31.5 million including Ireland) and Austria (36 million) all looked on in worry as the delicate power balance was thrown seriously out of kilter. Geographically, the new nation also seemed a colossus. Bismarck had ruthlessly used the victory in the Franco-Prussian War and annexed Alsace and Lorraine. The two French provinces had long since attracted the attention of the nationalist movement due to the German-speaking populations that lived there side-by-side with their French neighbours. In private, Bismarck repeatedly expressed doubts over the wisdom of such a move as he believed it would make reconciliation with France an impossibility and thus expose the young German nation state to foreign hostility from the outset. On the other hand, there had been popular demand to incorporate at least Alsace into the German Empire as its population was linguistically and culturally still overwhelmingly German. Bismarck eventually concluded that the 'hereditary hostility' (*Erbfeindschaft*) between France and Germany was inevitable and that one additional land dispute was neither here nor there. The twenty-five German states now stretched from the River Memel in the east to well beyond the River Rhine in the west; from the sea in the north to the Alps in the south – a German Empire indeed.

As intimidating as the bellicose foundation and the size and shape of the new Germany were, Bismarck tried his best to assure doubters that this was a progressive and peaceful nation. He designed a political system that tried to achieve this by balancing the many conflicting interests in Germany and Europe. It inevitably had serious flaws that have been criticised by generations of historians with the benefit of hindsight. The so-called *Sonderweg* theory, which has it that Germany followed a unique historical path when compared to other European nations, has now widely been discredited. However, many still like to see the journey from Bismarck's Germany to Hitler

The German Empire, 1871 - 1918

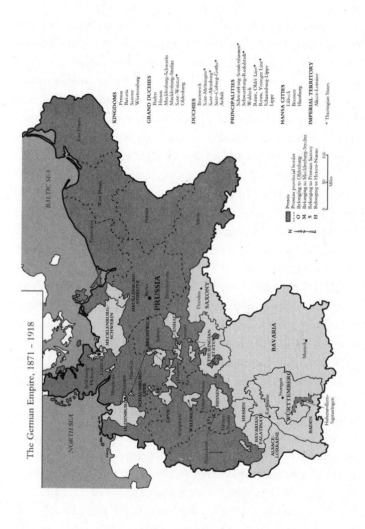

NORTH SEA

BALTIC SEA

East Prussia

Pomerania   West Prussia

PRUSSIA   Posen

Berlin   Brandenburg

Silesia

MECKLENBURG-   Stralsund
SCHWERIN

MECKLENBURG-
STRELITZ

SCHAUMBURG-
LIPPE

OLDENBURG   BREMEN   Hamburg

BRUNSWICK   ANHALT
                   Saxony

LIPPE

WALDECK   Dresden

HESSEN   Weißenfels   SAXONY

Kassel   THURINGIAN
                STATES

HESSEN   Frankfurt

BAVARIAN
PALATINATE   Karlsruhe   BAVARIA

ALSACE-   Stuttgart   Munich
LORRAINE

BADEN   WÜRTTEMBERG

Hohenzollern-
Sigmaringen

KINGDOMS
    Prussia
    Bavaria
    Saxony
    Württemberg

GRAND DUCHIES
    Baden
    Hessen
    Mecklenburg-Schwerin
    Mecklenburg-Strelitz
    Saxe-Weimar*
    Oldenburg

DUCHIES
    Brunswick
    Saxe-Meiningen*
    Saxe-Altenburg*
    Saxe-Coburg-Gotha*
    Anhalt

PRINCIPALITIES
    Schwarzburg-Sondershausen*
    Schwarzburg-Rudolstadt*
    Waldeck
    Reuss, Older Line*
    Reuss, Younger Line*
    Schaumburg-Lippe
    Lippe

HANSA CITIES
    Lübeck
    Bremen
    Hamburg

IMPERIAL TERRITORY
    Alsace-Lorraine

* Thuringian States

Prussia
O   Prussian provincial border
    Belonging to Oldenburg
M   Belonging to Mecklenburg-Strelitz
S   Belonging to Prussian Saxony
H   Belonging to Hessen-Nassau

0   50   100
    Miles

and the Holocaust as a straight line. Even well-established historians in the field, such as Neil MacGregor, describe 1871 as the beginning of Germany's 'Descent' into the next seventy-five 'dark years'.* When the Allied victors of the Second World War decided to abolish Prussia as a German state in 1947 as if exorcising a demon, they perpetuated the myth of the inevitability of the path from a Prussian-dominated Germany to Nazism. It is not only a simplistic narrative that fails to take into account the complexities of historical contexts but also one that sees individuals as mere passengers of historical currents with no agency over events. Bismarck had an impossible task in finding the lowest common denominator between a multitude of conflicting interests, and the fact that his constitution lasted for forty-seven years is nothing short of remarkable. Of course, the system was inherently flawed, but it did not set Germany upon an inevitable path to war and genocide.

On 3 March 1871 elections were held for the first-ever all-German parliament. All men over the age of 25 were eligible to vote irrespective of wealth or status. It has often been claimed that Bismarck only granted universal male suffrage because he hoped that the German people, who were still overwhelmingly rural with traditionalist views, would return a conservative parliament that would in turn cook up a constitution to Bismarck's political taste. In reality, the set-up of the German state had already been decided, and Bismarck was under no illusion that the recent unification process would produce anything other than a National Liberal victory. As predicted, the National Liberal Party indeed won the day with a vote share of 32.7 per cent, but this was no bad thing for Bismarck. With their power base in Prussia, these were mostly the very same people he had worked

---

*   MacGregor, p.375.

with in the North German Confederation, and it was therefore clear to all sides that the new constitution would not differ much from its predecessor. On 14 April 1871, it was ratified with an overwhelming majority. Germany had been 'put in the saddle', as Bismarck put it. Now it just needed to learn how to ride.

Imperial Constitution of 1871

The system that underpinned the Reich was an extremely fragile balancing act that tried to appease all interest groups. Naturally, Germany had to be set up as a federal state with significant powers for the twenty-five individual states, called *Länder*. However, Bismarck was also keen to preserve the central status of Prussia in the process, as he had promised Wilhelm. The result was a bicameral structure where the Prussian king would always be the German Kaiser in a personal union. Also, Prussia held seventeen votes in the upper chamber of parliament, the Bundesrat, where only fourteen votes were needed to veto any draft law. This chamber held representatives from each state, varying in number according to size. Thus an inbuilt insurance policy for Prussia had been achieved where even the combined agreement of all other states was not enough to pass laws that would be to its disadvantage. Besides, the Kaiser was the formal head of state. He had to give approval to all legislation and was commander-in-chief of the armed forces. As the Prussian king permanently held this position, this arrangement effectively preserved Prussian domination of the union. However, with all states represented in the Bundesrat, there seemed to be enough of a forum for the southern states to stay in the Reich. Serious and sustained mass secession movements have not to this day emerged at any time since Bismarck's skilful unification.

Another compromise had to be found between democracy and dynastic power. The ceremony at Versailles was intentionally set up as a show of the latter. Where Friedrich Wilhelm had turned down the German crown the 1848 revolutionaries had offered him because this came from the 'gutter', as he had put it, the one given to his brother by a collective of the German princes seemed somewhat more palatable. Again, historians have often viewed the proclamation ceremony with modern, republican eyes, seeing it as the machinations of an oppressive old elite that did not want to make way for progress. In truth, monarchical rule was still the norm in Europe, and most people deemed a decision-making process that was led from above as right and proper. Despite universal male suffrage, just over 50 per cent of eligible voters turned out for the first general election in March 1871. This was not, as some have argued, because the German people were sceptical of their new system but simply because democracy, politicisation and urbanisation were still a long way off the levels they would reach just a few years later. Society was still mostly traditional and rural. Introducing full male suffrage thus appeased the liberals and early socialists without threatening the elites too much, but what seemed a workable solution in 1871 would come to haunt Bismarck in the 1880s, where endless battles with parliament awaited him.

The Reichstag was the lower chamber where the elected representatives of the public took their seats. Bismarck was careful not to give it too much power as he was cautious to avoid mob rule, as most of the elites still saw it. So the Reichstag could not initiate legislation, and it could be dissolved by the Kaiser whenever he saw fit. Chancellor and Kaiser, therefore, dictated the direction of the Reich. There was also no accountability of the chancellor or the monarch to parliament; the chancellor answered only to the Kaiser, and the Kaiser answered only to God. However, Reichstag approval was needed to pass laws and crucially also budgetary matters, which meant Bismarck had to draft legislation and spending plans accordingly, often giving concessions to get it passed. This give-and-take between the legislative and executive branches of government was, at least in principle, a healthy sign of democracy that often frustrated the chancellor. In practice, Bismarck usually held the upper hand, using dubious tactics that ranged from tearful tirades to bullying and nepotism to get laws passed. If legend is to be believed, he lived his political life by the maxim that 'Laws are like sausages. It's best not to see them being made.'

Most of the weaknesses of this set-up came from the inherent paradoxes of the German Empire, not from Bismarck's deliberate attempts to frustrate the constitutional process. Was it possible to keep all twenty-five states in the union without sacrificing Prussian power? How can there be democracy without a threat to the elites' monopoly on decision making? These were difficult balancing acts that were skilfully managed by the Iron Chancellor. Bismarck could not make disappear the stark cultural rifts of a people that had been fractured for so long. Differences of regional loyalties, culture, custom, dialect, religion, history and (increasingly) social status would eventually fade and be replaced by a carefully managed concept of nationhood. But it would take time, and a good deal more blood and iron, before German national identity would begin to mature and stabilise.

Strange Bedfellows: Bismarck and the National Liberals

'Never has a statesman [...] had as his partner a political party so easy to deal with,'* wrote a disillusioned Max Weber in 1918 about the cooperation between Bismarck and the National Liberal Party in the so-called 'Liberal Era' from 1871 to 1878. The sociologist and philosopher was a great observer of the times he lived through and, writing here during the bitter end phase of a terrible, industrial war, his reflections on where and if liberalism in Germany went wrong are particularly pertinent. When the National Liberal Party was founded in 1867, it was made up of pragmatics with the aim of breaking the deadlock that had ensued between Bismarck and parliament in the so-called 'constitutional conflict'. Progressive idealists had demanded a more liberal–democratic set-up for the North German Confederation, but Bismarck blocked this. The National Liberals believed that it was best to work with the Iron Chancellor to achieve as much liberal change as possible so long as their popular position was still strong. This had not changed when the Reich was founded in 1871, and evidently, the compromise position also seemed popular with voters. Returning as the largest party from the first-ever elections, there was excellent bargaining potential for the National Liberals.

---

*   Max Weber Reflects on Cooperation between the National Liberals and Bismarck during the 1860s and 1870s (May 1918).

Still, as Max Weber observed, Bismarck overshadowed the system so much with his personality, his controlling style and his kudos as a political genius that it stifled the liberals and forced them into acting as a pressure group rather than a legislative partner. A liberal nationalist himself, Weber acknowledged that much was won and gained during the years of collaboration, but he also admitted that Bismarck perhaps had it too easy when it came to liberal support.

When one thinks of the bitter enmity between the liberals and the Prussian aristocracy in the 1848 revolution, exemplified perfectly by Bismarck's spontaneous arming of the local peasantry when he heard of the barricades in Berlin, it is difficult to imagine that the political aims of both groups would ever stand in alignment. But they did in 1871, and it is easy to see why. Nationalism once again showed its unifying potential. With the constitution ratified, it was Bismarck's next task in the spring of 1871 to begin unifying the economic infrastructure of his new realm so that a true common market could be set up. Just like Weber himself, most National Liberals were ardent capitalists, patriots, Prussians, Protestants and members of the rising middle classes. Thus a unified German economy with a common currency, measuring units, banking system, infrastructure network and free movement suited them just as much as it did the Reich Chancellor, who wanted all of these things as vehicles to stretch Prussian tentacles into the recently unified states. A somewhat cynical, yet fruitful alliance was formed that helped Bismarck pass most of his legislation in the early 1870s and set up the Reich's economy. The coalition passed a standard civil and criminal code for the whole Empire. It brought about the adoption of the gold standard while further stimulating the economy by abolishing all internal tariffs. Social and economic gains were made by investment in infrastructure – the railway network doubled from 1871 to 1890, which not only moved goods and raw materials around but also people. Urbanisation, job mobility and even early forms of commuting all meant that people were on the move, intermixing and overcoming their regional differences. The Reichsbank was also created, which helped regulate cash circulation and control. The common Protestantism of both parties also worked well as a bond when it came to suppressing Catholicism in Germany, and the Liberals became a reliable ally to Bismarck in the so-called *Kulturkampf*. But, of course, the harmony between such strange bedfellows would not last long. While there had been verbal clashes in the Reichstag between Bismarck and the National Liberals from the start, the first time the latter put their foot down and drove a hard bargain was in the army budget crisis of 1874.

Command over the army lay with the Kaiser, but financing it had to be approved by the Reichstag. When this conflict last arose in 1862, it nearly drove Wilhelm I into abdication and got Bismarck appointed as Minister President. But the latter was keen to avoid such spectacle this time and was thus ready for a compromise. When the deal of 1866–67 had been struck, and Bismarck's unlawful military reforms were retrospectively acknowledged as legitimate, the *junker* had to promise that he would henceforth respect the constitution and request renewed approval in 1872. However, he could not help himself and used the Franco-Prussian War to delay the legalisation of the budget once more until 1874. This time the matter could not be postponed, and so Bismarck opted for different tactics – he would simply set the negotiation bar extremely high. He put a draft forward that suggested a so-called 'Eternal Law'. This was an attempt to permanently fund a standing army of 400,000 that would need no further approval by the Reichstag. Ever. This was madness. It would have cost the equivalent of 80 per cent of all federal expenditure and with the budget the only real political lever at the Reichstag's disposal, it would then only have 20 per cent of this to work with. Bismarck knew, of course, that this was unacceptable, but it meant that the National Liberals had to move quite far over to meet him in the middle. After much rhetorical bluster where the parliamentarians half-heartedly demanded an annual review of military funds, Bismarck eventually threatened to dissolve the Reichstag and call new elections. Not brave enough to call Bismarck's bluff, the National Liberals negotiated a compromise, the so-called Septennates. This meant the budget would be fixed for seven years, which was longer than the lifespan of each parliament but not eternal. Here was a fitting example of Bismarck's constitution in action. This system gave elected parliamentarians enough power to curb or alter legislation brought forward by the executive but not so much as to force its hand. Had Bismarck dissolved the Reichstag, chances are the public would simply have voted the liberals back in and the stalemate might have resumed. But as Weber said, they made it comparatively easy for the Iron Chancellor.

When Bismarck's break with the National Liberal Party eventually came in 1878, it was for several reasons. Firstly, they had lost some thirty Reichstag seats in the election that year, which meant that a majority could be formed with the conservative parties. Secondly, Bismarck now saw a more dangerous adversary emerge, and he could not be sure of the support of the liberals in this matter: socialism was on the rise among the growing number of urban workers. Their demands for more democracy and rights overlapped at least partially with those of the liberals, and the conservatives seemed a more dependable ally in this respect. By this point, the Reich's economic policy was steering away from free trade and towards protectionism, which was, of course, anathema to the liberals and instead needed conservative backing. Most importantly, however, Bismarck had simply no use for liberalism any more. Having railroaded a liberal unification programme through the

Reichstag in the early 1870s, he had exhausted the common political ground. New things had to be tackled, and so new allies were needed. Bismarck was in full realpolitikal flow when he set about destroying his old ally.

Using his silver tongue and some political scheming, Bismarck managed to split the once-mighty liberal movement into those who were willing to work with him to achieve at least some of their aims and those who could not bring themselves to let their principles slip any further. The latter group seceded from the party and joined the Progress Party, which would turn into the German Radical Party in 1884. Votes divided, liberalism became a muted movement in Germany while the Social Democrats were beginning to put some serious pressure on the government. It was a sign of how much nationalism and liberalism were intertwined in nineteenth-century Germany. A robust movement from the Liberation Wars in 1812 onwards, it grew so confident that it came close to toppling the existing order in 1848–49. Nonetheless, the movement burnt itself out as it fulfilled many of its aims. Most Germans were content with a constitutional monarchy, and they adored both Bismarck and Wilhelm I for all their faults. Political theory and idealism could not yet contend with charisma and royal authority. When the movement had few original demands left, it became less relevant to the voting public, and Bismarck simply provided the final push. German liberalism would not recover from this decline for decades to come and it was in this melancholy context that Max Weber wrote his reflections in 1918, at which point socialists, communists and right-wing nationalists all made louder noises of opposition. The second German Revolution of 1918 would not be dominated by liberalism.

A German Caesar? Governance of the Reich

Kaiser Wilhelm complained that it was 'hard to be king under Bismarck'. How could he be a sovereign, answerable only to God, and yet allow himself to be bullied and manipulated by a crazy *junker* who had come out of nowhere and taken politics by storm? Unsure about the path he was being taken on, Wilhelm had not approved of any of the major decisions that were made from the moment he had appointed Bismarck as Minister President of Prussia in 1862. He was so frightened of the liberal majority in parliament, who had just shot down his military reforms, that he seriously contemplated abdication in September 1862. He had watched on in horror as Bismarck coolly told the assembled MPs that he would take Prussia on a path of 'iron and blood' whether they liked it or not. Similarly, when it was time to unify the Reich and Wilhelm was reluctant to give up his Prussian crown, even in tears over the matter on the very morning of the proclamation of the German Empire on 18 January 1871, he somehow went along with Bismarck's scheme, never entirely sure why. The Iron Chancellor exerted a tremendous amount of control over his contemporaries, enemies and allies alike, and he did so without the oratorical fireworks of twentieth-century dictators. In 1909, *Grieben's Travel Guide to Berlin* claimed that even Bismarck's statue in the capital still radiated the 'unyielding willpower that reflected in his powerful posture and in the expression of his sparkling eyes' – eleven years after the chancellor's death. An inherent and unshakable conviction that he was doing the right thing and would not be deterred from it surrounded Bismarck and had a great effect on parliamentarians, foreign diplomats and even the king. This was the characteristic that made him one of the greatest statesmen of all time.

Both contemporaries and historians have described Bismarck's political style as dictatorial, even 'Caesaristic'. It is easy to see why modern observers have strong reservations about the central position he gave himself as chancellor in the constitution. He set up a German tradition of a 'chancellor democracy' that (despite considerable variation) has survived wars, dictatorships, division and reunification. At the time of writing, Angela Merkel is in her fourth term as German chancellor, still with high approval ratings, and follows in the footsteps of other long-serving predecessors such as Helmut Kohl and Konrad Adenauer. The language Germans use for their chancellors reflects the central role the position plays in the national psyche. Where Bismarck was the 'Gründervater' (founding father), Angela Merkel is affectionately known as 'Mutti Merkel'. It seems a nation so fractured and diverse, so scarred by division, war and bitter memories, craves stability and leadership in an almost childlike way. The idea of an authoritative father figure appeals in this context and Bismarck fitted the role perfectly.

The French Revolution and its aftermath had triggered long-lasting shifts in political thinking in Europe. After 1848 even the staunchest supporters of monarchical rule began to accept a degree of constitutional moderation of royal power. But developments in France had also shown that dictatorial power and progressive values were not mutually exclusive concepts. Napoleon's introduction of the Code Civil in 1807 and its reintroduction in 1853 under Napoleon III had shown that unelected leadership did not have to be entirely at odds with liberal ideas and the rule of law. Thus the concept of a 'modern' dictatorship was hotly debated in the mid- and late nineteenth century and had supporters even in liberal circles. After the fall of Napoleon III in the course of the Franco–Prussian War in 1870, many liberals believed that the new German nation state might be able to achieve what France had not: to secure freedom for all through a king who would defend the rule of law without succumbing to despotism. The trouble was that the ruling classes despised this concept. The very idea that they would be tied to a civil code in the same way as every common man and woman smacked of revolution and republicanism. A bigger problem still was that 'Caesarism', as political thinkers called it even then, required a charismatic and popular leader, such as Napoleon had been. But Wilhelm I was no Bonaparte or Caesar. He was liked well enough by many Germans, but, still, he did not have the almost mesmerising quality that Napoleon had radiated when he convinced the French nation to vote for a return of absolute power.

Bismarck was no great orator either, at least not when it came to the quality and resonance of his voice. Historian Volker Ullrich describes Bismarck's 'jerky, tentative manner of speaking' and his 'thin, reedy voice'* but also notes that this did not mean that his speech lacked impact. He more than made up for the quality of his voice by the precision and colourful nature of his register. Even in his early school reports, his teachers described Bismarck's eloquence as astonishing. Using exceptionally evocative verbal images, he found it easy to provoke, irritate, soothe or charm even his most hostile adversaries. His distinctive physique further enhanced his impact. He was a bear of a man at 6ft 2in height with a barrel chest, blond hair and an equally blond iconic moustache. When this huge man walked into the room, self-assured and steely-eyed, people stopped to listen. The Iron Chancellor had also carefully built his own legend in the course of his career. Starting out as an eccentric aristocrat, then clashing with established parliamentarians, diplomats and revolutionaries in the 1840s,

---

★   Ullrich, *Bismarck*, p.33.

he quickly gained a reputation for being 'iron' before he put the words to it himself in his famous 1862 speech. By the time he had instigated and won the unification wars, he had become a national hero.

Otto von Bismarck, *c.*1875.

Kaiser Wilhelm himself had an odd relationship with Bismarck. Initially reluctant to appoint him as Minister President when he took over as King of Prussia in 1861, it had taken the crisis of the military reforms in 1862 for him to recall Bismarck from Paris. But Wilhelm quickly became dependent on his ferocious advisor. Changing the words and actions of the king in the Ems Telegram was an outrageous act in terms of both diplomacy and personal trust. Yet Wilhelm saw no way to defy Bismarck. Once the German Empire was formed in 1871, Wilhelm lost interest in the day-to-day affairs of central government. He was the King of Prussia and never wanted to be German Kaiser. That was what Bismarck wanted, and that was what he should get. So Wilhelm withdrew more and more to his Prussian palaces and rural retreats where he hunted, invited guests and took little interest in the running of his new Reich. Bismarck was no republican, and he had the highest respect for the institution of the monarchy. Still, he had set up his new constitution in such a way that it allowed the Head of State to leave the running of the country to him as chancellor much in the same way that a shop owner might choose to appoint a manager and rarely enter the shop again. If there was a German Caesar, it was Bismarck, not Wilhelm.

As a realpolitiker, Bismarck also had no moral qualms about doing whatever was required to get his laws passed. The famous 'laws are like sausages' analogy that is often attributed to him hit the nail on the head – the process of making laws in the Second Reich was indeed messy and unpalatable. Bismarck had a full repertoire of methods to bully, cajole and badger parliamentarians and the king into submission. Nothing was off-limits. When his finely tuned rhetoric would not do the trick, Bismarck could throw intimidating tantrums, humiliate adversaries in public, burst into tears or – in very deserving cases – threaten to resign.* The thought that Wilhelm might be left to run a German Empire that was entirely anathema to his Prussian soul frightened the ageing king so much that he would promise Bismarck almost anything so long as he stayed by his side.

Bismarck controlled every aspect of government to the point of obsession. He micromanaged the affairs of senior cabinet members and the civil service, and found it very hard to delegate work or trust others to do a job properly. The upshot of this was a certain amount of nepotism in Bismarck's political circle. In 1874, he urged his eldest son Herbert to join the civil service and helped him befriend the king's grandson, Wilhelm, who would later become Wilhelm II. In 1886 Bismarck appointed Herbert as foreign secretary in order to have someone he trusted in this central office while Germany's position in Europe still had to be so carefully managed.

Bismarck's relationship with Queen Augusta had further deteriorated since he had tried to convince her to conspire against her brother-in-law, King Friedrich Wilhelm, during the 1848 revolution. Augusta found Bismarck an arrogant and unbearable man who had far too much influence over her husband. Her relationship with the German chancellor broke down so much that they refused to dine together in the same room, which must have been rather awkward for Kaiser Wilhelm. Bismarck also fell out with the king's daughter-in-law, Victoria. Crown Prince Friedrich had married his English wife in the hope that they could introduce a more liberal system of government in Germany that was modelled on the English constitution. Queen Victoria had also raised her eldest daughter to look up to her and her German consort Prince Albert for a model of how a queen could rule with her husband. Bismarck despised this notion, especially as it

---

*   See also Steinberg.

showed that Frederick would only reign in name while his wife would make the decisions. Historian Jonathan Steinberg goes a little far when he suggests that this hints towards a deep-rooted misogyny that Bismarck had supposedly harboured since childhood. Still, there is no doubt that he despised both Augusta and Victoria as meddling women who got in the way when he sought to manipulate their husbands. He simply abhorred the blot on his otherwise highly successful art of political persuasion.

In his role as chancellor, it was Bismarck's task to control the Reichstag. Constitutionally unable to initiate legislation, it nevertheless had the right to block the draft laws it was presented with and did so often. Bismarck had to come up with a bit more than tears and bluster to convince the 394 representatives to go along with his plans. The carefully managed alliances and backroom deals were skilfully counter-balanced with ruthless political schemes such as the destruction of the National Liberal Party. This is a crucial difference from the Bonaparte model of republican dictatorship. Neither of the two French emperors of the nineteenth century had to fight frustrating battles with a belligerent parliament. The whole point of concentrating the entire representation of the nation in one strong leader was to avoid the supposed weakness and division that comes with a multitude of opinions. In the eyes of both Napoleons, that was where the French Revolution had gone wrong. Bismarck did not have this luxury. Charismatic or not, he had to contend with the representatives of an increasingly politicised German people. Even though he only answered to the Kaiser, who in turn would never sack him, he had nevertheless created a system where laws could only be passed with the assent of the representatives of the German people.

Well liked but not exceptionally charismatic, Wilhelm I did not possess the essential ingredients to take on a Napoleonic role. More crucially still, he lacked interest in his new Reich, and his subjects sensed that. Had he tried to force his will on to the German people after 1871, this would have back-fired spectacularly. At first glance, the Caesarean image fits Bismarck somewhat better. His commanding aura and immense popularity gave him authority far beyond the con-straints of the constitution he had created. But he too would have found it impossible to rule without the consent of the people via their representatives in the Reichstag. Many Germans adored Bismarck as the blacksmith who forged their nation and they built him hundreds of memorials after his death. Still, the times were as much dominated by lib-eral and democratic thought as they were by nationalism and authoritarianism. As Markus Prutsch has shown, 'Despite his impressive plenitude of power, "disposability" was a charac-teristic feature of Bismarck's position throughout his career.'* This was hardly the position of a modern dictator. There was no German Caesar.

Kulturkampf: Bismarck and German Catholicism

The unification of Germany without Austria had far-reaching consequences for the religious composition of the newly formed nation. By excluding one of the largest Catholic areas of the German-speaking lands, Bismarck had effectively made Catholics a minority. Out of historical developments such as the Reformation and the Thirty Years' War, Germany emerged with a unique religious landscape. The northern German territories had primarily been established as Protestant while the south had

---

*   Prutsch, p.139.

remained Catholic. The Rhineland too was mostly Catholic, which had already led to significant tensions when it was allocated to Prussia in 1815. (Over a century later, prominent Rhinelanders such as Konrad Adenauer, later appointed West Germany's first chancellor in 1949, still campaigned to remove the Rhineland from Prussian control.) Now that Prussia had extended its reach over the south as well, there was significant concern among Catholics. The trauma of the Thirty Years' War, which had pitted German Protestants and Catholics against each other in a terrible civil war, had left deep scars on the collective German psyche, and the prospect of further religious conflict loomed large in 1871. In addition, the French Revolution and the subsequent Napoleonic reforms had sought to limit the influence of the Catholic Church in France and its satellite states, which included the Confederation of the Rhine. This radical secularisation sent shockwaves through Europe and triggered widespread discussion about the relationship between church and state. Liberals and progressives were bolstered in their calls for secularisation, which in turn triggered a defensive backlash from Catholic groups and the papacy. Church schools, clubs and societies all saw a rise in membership and demanded independence from the reaches of government. Ironically, the demand for freedom from state authority created a wave of political Catholicism.

In the context of German unification under Prussian and therefore Protestant leadership, it is no surprise that Catholics felt the need for political representation of their interests. Formed in December 1870, the *Deutsche Zentrumspartei* (Centre Party), was set up to defend German Catholicism against secularisation. Passing a programme that demanded decentralisation, independence for the Church and social reform, the committee declared that this was 'to combat the so-called Prussian traditions', revealing a deep mistrust towards the Prussian-led government that was being set up. The *Zentrum* had the potential to become a formidable force of opposition to Bismarck. As the only party that was not tied to social class, it appealed to all Catholics in Germany and thus to a third of all voters. If Bismarck did not tread carefully, a collective Catholic awakening in Germany could be channelled into political action through the Centre Party, which had already emerged as the second-largest party in the 1871 elections, gaining 18.6 per cent of the vote. This showed that most Catholics had voted for a party representing their religious interest rather than political, economic or social matters.

Bismarck felt he could not leave the matter be. He was also worried about the prospect of papal interference in the fragile German union he had just cobbled together. At the First Vatican Council of 1869–70, the Pope had formally issued the dogma of Papal Infallibility, which declared that as God's representative, his teachings never erred on any given matter and must thus be obeyed by all. In addition, Pius IX had issued the Syllabus of Errors in 1864, which denounced liberalism, nationalism and the separation of church and state as errors. Combined with Papal Infallibility then, this posed a serious conflict of interest to many German Catholics. The Pope had in effect declared that everything the new German state stood for was wrong. In other words, if German Catholics followed Bismarck's lead, they would act against papal doctrine and, by extension, God's will.

Bismarck was greatly concerned by this. It was only through war and clever tactics that he had managed to convince the Catholic states south of the River Main to join his proposed union. Besides, the Catholic Rhinelanders had proved to be as insubordinate as the Polish minorities in the east, who were still calling for secession. Since the Franco-Prussian war, he now also had Alsace and Lorraine to deal with. Bismarck felt he needed to get the situation under control if he wanted to hold his Reich together. It was, therefore, a tactical move to declare those who sought to undermine German unity *Reichsfeinde* – enemies of the state. The concept would even prove useful to Bismarck in other contexts as it conjured up the idea of an internal enemy to German unity that rallied all social classes behind a common goal. In peacetime, it seemed the next best unifying measure when external conflict was not on the cards. It helped that the liberals too were worried about political Catholicism. Pius had not only condemned liberalism as an ideology but with it all the fundamental rights it stood for, such as freedom of speech. Even during the German War against Austria in 1866, this had led to repeated skirmishes between German Catholics and Protestants that the military found difficult to control. Bismarck and his allies the National Liberals were therefore entirely in agreement that action was required in the name of German unity. They saw in it nothing less than a battle for the soul of the German nation, a *Kulturkampf*.

Bismarck thought the limitation of Catholic resistance was best achieved bureaucratically at first while state education and collective experiences would mould the nation together in the long run. A raft of measures was brought in to limit political Catholicism and separate church and state. In December 1871 the so-called 'Pulpit Paragraph' launched the first major attack. It forbade the expression of political opinions and criticism of the government in churches. This was complemented in March 1872 by a School Inspection Law, which allowed the state sole right to inspect and monitor schools, including private and confessional ones. This may not seem a drastic move, but given the long-standing clerical domination of education in Europe, it revealed a lot about the growing confidence of secular governments and the branching out of their power into the private domain of their subjects. For centuries the Catholic Church had accompanied people through every major step of their lives, regulating birth, marriage, death and everything in between. By taking over the moral and academic education of young Germans, Bismarck had triggered a culture struggle.

The chancellor tried to deflect some of the criticism of these early measures by arguing that the school inspections were only necessary because many Polish schools had refused to adopt German as the language of instruction, which in turn hindered the development of unity. It was certainly true that he was afraid of the Polish secession movement and wanted to control the education and assimilation of young Poles. But there is no doubt that the National Liberals saw a chance here to once and for all take education out of the reactionary hands of the Church and introduce a secular curriculum instead. That this was an ideological war and not just a pacification measure for Poland became glaringly obvious when the Reichstag passed a law in the summer of 1872 that expelled all Jesuits from Germany. There were only about 200 German Jesuits, but they were seen as the Pope's most loyal agents in the country, and the paranoia about papal interference with German politics had reached new heights. In turn, now fearing that more drastic measures were still to come, German Catholics responded with defiance and outrage. The anger, suspicion and fear reached boiling point in the spring of 1873. The stage was set for the *Kulturkampf* to be launched in earnest.

Now genuinely paranoid about a supposedly all-powerful reactionary movement called the 'Black International', Bismarck broke off all diplomatic relations with the Vatican and allowed his Minister of Education, Adalbert Falk, to introduce a radical set of measures, the so-called 'May Laws' of 1873. These subjugated the Church almost completely to state control. Clergymen were now required to have a degree from a German university, religious appointments had to be reported to state authorities, and a 'Royal Court for Clerical Matters' was introduced. Not content with controlling the Church politically, the liberal alliance removed state funding in 1875 to weaken religious structures financially. Bismarck and the National Liberals also sought to extend state control over the traditional areas of birth, marriage and death. In 1875, civil marriages were introduced as the only legal form. A couple could still get married in a church but only after they had had a state ceremony to make the marriage official in law. This shows very clearly that the *Kulturkampf* was not a mere measure to restrict Catholic political activity, but it was indeed a battle over spiritual and moral authority in Germany.

Given the severity of the measures, it is hardly surprising that they triggered an intense backlash from the Church. Instead of cowing German Catholics into submission, they only served to fire a spirit of solidarity. The *Zentrum* gained nearly 25 per cent of votes in the 1877 elections, meaning the vast majority of Catholics now voted for political representation of their faith. Protestants too felt aggrieved by the rapid and aggressive secularisation of society. The May Laws applied to Protestant institutions, schools and marriages just the same, which left Prussian conservatives just as unhappy and concerned as their Catholic counterparts. The religious element aside, the measures simply smacked of radical reform to many deeply conservative Germans who despised the moral and theological relativism of the liberal progressives. A godless and therefore amoral society was a spectre that frightened many. Towards the late 1870s, the *Kulturkampf* seemed increasingly a political dead end to Bismarck.

If Bismarck needed a further incentive to cut his losses and reconcile himself with German Catholics and conservatives, it helped that the liberal movement was in sharp decline. Economic factors also played a role as Bismarck came under immense pressure to introduce protective tariffs, which were complete anathema to the liberals and needed a conservative majority in the Reichstag. When the new Pope, Leo XIII, was elected in Rome in 1878 and immediately signified that he was ready for reconciliation, the timing seemed right. Ever the real-politiker, Bismarck ended his long alliance with the National Liberals and built a new majority in the Reichstag with the conservatives and the Centre Party, whom he convinced that it was worth forgetting their differences in the face of a new dangerous enemy: socialism.

Many have described the painful *Kulturkampf* as a political blunder and a rare example of bad judgement for Bismarck. It is true that the sudden paranoia of 1872–73 caused an overreaction that alienated many Germans and not just Catholics. Many of the May Laws had to be repealed, and to this day Catholicism has retained significant political influence, but the ultimate objective of the *Kulturkampf* – to change the relationship of church and state – was not a complete failure. The wheels had been set in motion for the creation of a secular society with nationhood, not denomination, as the highest cultural reference point. Marriages have remained a civil prerogative to this day, the vast majority of children attend state schools where religious education cannot be forced upon them, and religious life is seen as a private matter. The *Kulturkampf* may have overshot its targets with its aggressive and clumsy implementation. Still, the struggle was won by the liberals in the end and religion in Germany has played second fiddle to national identity ever since.

Made in Germany: The Reich Becomes an Economic Giant

Products labelled 'Made in Germany' are the most trusted in the world today.[*] This stems from a long German industrial history with a strong emphasis on exports. Initially, France and especially Britain had been able to industrialise and modernise at a much more rapid pace than the divided Germans, but from the mid-nineteenth century onwards it was time to catch up. First through the *Zollverein*, then the North German Confederation and lastly the newly unified Empire, there had been more and more economic cooperation in the German lands, leading to what economic historians have dubbed the Second Industrial Revolution.

Germany was naturally suited to industrialisation in a way that no other European country was. The geographical conditions are ideal. With access to the sea in the north, direct borders with many European neighbours, large and deep rivers like the Rhine, Danube, Elbe, Oder and Spree criss-crossing the land and flat plains ideal for railway tracks throughout the north, the only thing that hindered an efficient infrastructure and trade network was the lack of coordination between the German states up to 1871. In addition, Germany has vast resources of iron ore, coal and minerals alongside fertile agricultural land that provided enough food to sustain immense population growth. United, it was now the biggest European state in terms of both landmass and people and therefore had the potential to develop the largest economy. The conditions were ideal for making the new German Empire the envy of the world.

---

[*]   Made-in-Country-Index (MICI) 2017 Report.

And so it was that from 1871 Germany experienced what some have called a 'Foundation Boom', which had such a profound economic and social impact that the entire era became known as the *Gründerzeit* (literally: Founders' Period) with its distinct style of design, furniture and art. Berlin in particular experienced a huge building boom. Elegant houses with richly decorated facades were erected to accommodate the nouveaux riches and cater to their increased confidence. Most of these buildings in the capital fell victim to the extensive bombing of the Second World War but many stunning examples survived in other cities, such as the Hamburg City Hall and the iconic Neues Rathaus at the Marienplatz in Munich. The German victory in the Franco-Prussian War did much to aid the situation as France had agreed to pay 5 billion francs in reparations by March 1875. This provided a financial boost for investment in infrastructure such as railways, which were nationalised in Prussia and enjoyed colossal cash injections. By 1880, Germany's railways were transporting 43,000 passengers annually and had superseded the French system.* Unlike other European countries, Germany did not focus on passenger transport, however, but on getting raw materials and industrial output from A to B. Thus the industrial heartlands of the Ruhr were favoured and received a dense network of crisscrossing lines with fast connections to the ports of Hamburg and Bremen in the north. Though the focus on industry left rural communities isolated, it helped the German economy catch up with its rivals with blinding speed. Heavy industry quickly utilised this transport network together with a growing labour force. The production of so-called pig iron (a versatile raw iron product intended for remelting) alone rose by 61 per cent between 1870 and 1872, and even this was not

---

*   Mitchell, p.178.

enough as demand outnumbered this figure vastly, increasing by 111 per cent. This, in turn, pushed up the prices for pig iron by 90 per cent* and so led to higher profit margins that could be reinvested into subsidiary industries such as construction, machinery and manufacturing.

Between the immediate economic effect of the unification and the jubilant mood of nationalism that followed the victories of 1870, the impact on German economic confidence was immense. People felt their new nation state was capable of anything. A new and spectacular Reichstag building was commissioned to embody this spirit. After 103 architects submitted their ideas in 1872, the winning entry foresaw a neo-baroque structure with a steel-and-glass cupola, only possible due to the latest developments in engineering. Philadelphia's Memorial Hall and London's Crystal Palace had previously captured the world's imagination and now it was Germany's time to shine. Thus vast amounts of money were being invested in the full expectation that the economy would continue to grow at such rapid pace. There had been very little economic regulation as Bismarck and his liberal allies favoured a free market policy right from the outset. Appointing the sober and efficient bureaucrat Rudolph von Delbrück as President of the new German Reich Chancellery, Bismarck had chosen a trusted free-marketeer to establish the unified German market. Delbrück had already acted in this capacity in the North German Confederation and became Bismarck's right-hand man. This meant in 1871 there was almost no regulation of financial conduct. Large monopolies and cartels formed as well as corporations such as Deutsche Bank and Commerzbank – both still major players today. The feverish economic atmosphere of the *Gründerzeit*

---

*   LeMO.

led to the massive investment of private money into the mushrooming industry, and share prices rose by 50 per cent on average. When it had finally reached saturation point in 1873 and a wave of hysteria swept through Europe's financial markets, this all came to a crashing halt. The Great Panic of 1873 reached Berlin in October and triggered Germany's first recession.

In many ways, this first economic crisis did not harm German industry in the medium and long term. It merely levelled what had been an overheated and unhealthy amount of growth in the first couple of years of the Reich. Growth rates stagnated but did not fall drastically, and production rates normalised, preventing overproduction problems on the scale seen in other countries. Nonetheless, the middle and working classes were particularly vulnerable to these economic currents. Some of the agricultural labourers who had flocked to the cities, where they earned decent wages as industrial workers, suddenly found themselves unemployed. With no welfare cushion to soften the impact and displaced from supportive family networks, they now fell into poverty and squalor. Alone and homeless, they roamed the cold streets of German cities, looking for casual work and begging for scraps of food. This was a far cry from the modern life in the city that they had come for. The middle classes, who had made their fortunes in investment and banking over the last two years, had also often lost everything as they had no physical assets to see them through a financial crisis. Cramped into cheap, small tenement housing, they dreamt of a return to better times. It was in this context that many Germans became disillusioned with liberal free-market policies. Anger at the fat cats in banking swiftly turned into demands for political action to control them. The days of laissez-faire capitalism in Germany were numbered and liberals like Delbrück had to go.

Bismarck had no strong views on economic policy either way, but pressure on him was mounting. The worldwide over-production of grain had led to cheap imports from Russia, Argentina and the USA undercutting German agriculture. Powerful pressure groups such as the Central Association of German Industrialists had also begun to form and demanded more protection for German industry.* Bismarck had no choice but to change course. Loyal old Delbrück was the first victim of this when he was pushed out of office in 1876 after over a decade of service for Bismarck. He also needed to abandon the National Liberals in the Reichstag as they would never have approved of a course of economic protectionism. The situation was ripe for Bismarck to jump the liberal ship and board a conservative one.

Ironically it was the anti-Catholic aggression of the Bismarck regime during the *Kulturkampf* that had bolstered votes for the Centre Party, which came out of the 1878 elections with 23.1 per cent. The German Reich Party and the German Conservative Party together now also made up 27 per cent of the Reichstag. Meanwhile, the National Liberal vote had collapsed with a loss of nearly a quarter of their seats. Promising the Catholics and the conservative parties a coalition for protectionist economic policy and against socialism and liberalism, Bismarck had somehow managed to convince his enemies of yesterday that the *Kulturkampf* should just be forgiven and forgotten. It worked, and a majority bloc was created in parliament that passed a Tariff Act on 12 June 1879. This introduced a customs duty of 10 marks per tonne of imported pig iron, increasing the price of it by 17 per cent and thereby making it much more expensive than the German product. In agriculture too, wheat now carried a customs duty

---

*   Kitchen, p.146.

of 70 marks per tonne,* making Bismarck's *junker* friends with their large land estates very happy. The so-called Marriage of Iron and Rye, a combined lobby group of new and old elites, now formed a mighty power bloc in the 1880s that would dominate economic policy and by extension social policy for decades to come.

While the significance of agriculture as an economic sector overall had shrunk in comparison with industry, the growth rates caused by mechanisation and better technology were nonetheless staggering. Between 1873 and 1913, wheat production grew by over 50 per cent, and the number of pigs reared also increased from 7 million to 25 million, chiefly due to the introduction of sodium nitrate as fertiliser and steam-driven machinery. Economically this drastic increase in production had two significant effects. One, overproduction led to a price and wage slump that made agriculture an unattractive sector to work in. Two, there was now plenty of food to go around, and this was less dependent on fluctuations in weather and harvest. With a stable and plentiful supply of nourishment, the German population grew rapidly, reaching nearly 50 million by the end of Bismarck's tenure in 1890. This, in turn, provided a sizable domestic market and a larger workforce, both of which contributed further to economic growth.

It was not just the traditional sectors of iron, coal and agriculture that grew. As crucial to Germany in the medium and long term were its new industries of chemicals, electrical goods and mechanical engineering. German exports in machinery alone increased sixfold between 1871 and 1913, with the 'Made in Germany' concept beginning to be associated with well-made, durable and innovative products. This sector

---

*   LeMO.

alone accounted for 7 per cent of exports. Early combustion engines and even the first cars in the 1880s foreshadowed the path that would take the German economy from the 1870s to the present, irrespective of the disruption and catastrophe of two world wars. The electrical sector, too, proved durable. Some of the most successful German companies established themselves in Bismarck's Reich, such as Siemens and AEG, which began to supply companies at first and then entire cities with electricity. Last but by no means least, chemical giants such as BASF and Bayer that still dominate today's market also contributed to Germany's economic growth. What these new industries brought to the table was a vast and lucrative field of highly specialised and innovative output. They required an educated and skilled workforce, which in turn was in a position to demand high wages and good working conditions. Due to the high level of specialisation, the products on offer had little international competition and could not easily be undercut. Given the quality and reputation of Germany's exports, prices remained high and brought in significant revenue for industrialists, workers and state.

The new German state was in an ideal position to create a strong economic empire even without the advantage of a worldwide network of colonies that could be exploited for resources and manpower. The fact that Germany had come too late to the imperialist party and had thus missed out on the chance to develop an empire on the scale of that of Britain or France did not seem to hold the young nation back economically. The brief setback of 1873 did not bring down the fledgling economy but instead pruned the overgrowth of the *Gründerzeit*. Switching from free trade to protectionism, Germany developed into a modern industrial giant that began to rival its Western European neighbours.

What is German? Society in Bismarck's Reich

When in 1878, the famous German composer Richard Wagner attempted to answer the question, 'What is German?', it was a matter that he had been pondering since 1865. Thirteen years on, he still concluded that he was 'unqualified for further answering the question: *was ist Deutsch*?'* While perhaps best known for his operas such as *The Ring of the Nibelung*, Wagner also became an influential public figure due to his political activism and his eccentric lifestyle. His turbulent marriage with actress Minna Planer, with whom he fled to London and Paris to escape the debts that he had accumulated wherever he went, made him as infamous as his anti-Semitic polemic. But he was also actively involved in early socialist movements as well as the revolutions of 1848–49. Like so many German nationalists, he felt somewhat disillusioned with what had been achieved by the end of the first decade of the German Empire. Wagner's fight on the barricades in 1848–49 and the time served in political exile in the aftermath of that revolution had all seemed worth it when his fatherland was finally united in 1871. But by 1878 a certain cynicism had set in: 'My German heart leaped high, too, when liberally we voted for "Free-trade": there was, and still prevails, much want throughout the land; the workman hungers, and industry has fallen sick: but "business" flourishes.'† Wagner is typical of the first generation of 'Germans' who had such high hopes for their new society in 1871 and who would feel uncertain and even disaffected when the glorious unity they had envisioned clashed with the reality of Bismarck's Reich.

Initially, most Germans were optimistic about their futures in the new German Empire. As historian Michael Stürmer has

---

*   Wagner, p.169.
†   Ibid.

shown, rapid industrialisation brought about rapid progress, which meant most people looked forward to 'longer and happier lives' and expected their children to have it even better.[*] The so-called *Fortschrittsoptimismus* (literally 'progress optimism') was palpable in all layers of society between 1871 and 1873, so much so that the American historian Fritz Stern even spoke of 'national intoxication' and 'unrestrained hubris'.[†] On an individual level, too, many Germans could look to real evidence of progress. Their wages rose, new jobs appeared, and Germans like Robert Koch rivalled Europe's best in the field of medicine. Germany had been set on a path of greatness as far as many of its citizens were concerned, and national sentiment rode high.

The financial crisis of 1873 damped such optimism considerably. Where the bourgeois-capitalist-liberal way of doing things had seemed a straight path to German greatness and progress, suspicions now grew that it was a system that only benefited a small clique of businessmen and bankers while the rest of society was being left behind. As with Richard Wagner himself, this could often take on the form of anti-Semitic tropes in claims that it was, in fact, Jewish financiers who sought to divide Germany for their own benefit. The year 1873 certainly caused a conservative backlash against liberalism that took hold in all social classes. At the top, members of the old aristocracy saw their fears confirmed that land ownership and titles no longer guaranteed wealth and political influence. Mechanisation, mass production and competition from industry had seriously begun to undermine their status in society. At the lower end of the social hierarchy, the working classes were struggling with the fallout from the so-called 'long depression' that began in 1873 and lasted into the 1880s. The German economy had not been hit as hard as

---

[*]   Sturmer, Ch. 2.

[†]   Stern, p.50.

comparable Western countries such as the USA, but nonetheless low appetite for investment often meant terrible working conditions. With little protection by way of welfare, health and safety and employment law, workers were dependent on the goodwill (or often lack thereof) of their employers, who now sought to maximise their profit margins ruthlessly. While wages still rose across the period and economic expansion continued regardless of the 1873 crash, the cost of living increased sharply, economic historian Gerhard Bry estimates by around 14 per cent between 1871 and 1874, before it began to drop back to more manageable levels. But by then, a culture of exploitation had set in, and the developments of urbanisation and proletarianisation had created a large and angry underclass. The workers' dreams of a glorious fatherland had inadvertently led to them being trapped in an economic and social position they could not escape no matter how hard they worked. Partially as a result of this disillusionment, the rate of German emigration to America nearly doubled from the 1870s to the 1880s,* although this also included many Catholics fleeing persecution in the context of the *Kulturkampf*.

Irrespective of the financial crisis of 1873, the long-term process of urbanisation, which was accelerated as a side effect of the Second Industrial Revolution, posed its own challenges. As the new capital of the Reich, Berlin may be an extreme example, but its figures give an idea of the scale of the movement of people. Having already experienced a boom as the capital of Prussia and then the North German Confederation, Berlin was Germany's largest city in 1871, with 913,984 inhabitants. By the end of Bismarck's tenure in 1890, the figure had more than doubled as 1.9 million people called Berlin their home. Most Germans still lived in rural areas (even by 1910, only one-fifth of the population

---

*   *2008 Yearbook of Immigration Statistics*. Office of Immigration Statistics. US Department of Homeland Security.

lived in large cities), but the trend was set. Local authorities tried their best to regulate infrastructure and house building. Still, the rules were often established before the urbanisation boom really hit and were thus inadequate to deal with the scale of the problem. Berlin suffered even more than other cities, with a population density twice that of the urbanised Ruhr region. Thus the phenomenon of the *Berliner Mietskaserne* emerged. The closest translation to English is 'tenement'. The terms are indeed similar in that they refer to rented accommodation where the inhabitants would occupy one small part of the building, i.e. a flat or a room, rather than the entire house. But in German, *Kaserne* also means 'barracks' and it conjured up a dreary image of spartan, monotonous and cramped living conditions. Regulations for planning permission were minimal, and the urgency of the situation demanded quick, cheap housing, not comfort. Thus rows and rows of anonymous housing blocks emerged with inadequate ventilation, outside space and hygiene precautions. The result was dark and damp living that had to be shared with multiple family members or colleagues. The *Mietskaserne* was thus synonymous with the plight of the working classes in the cities, particularly in Berlin and Hamburg where conditions were worst. Poets such as Arno Holz (nominated for the Nobel Prize in Literature nine times) were fascinated by the darkness and squalor of such places:

> Its roof thrust up almost to the stars,
> The factory from the courtyard drones,
> This is what the real Mietskaserne was
> Complete with hurdy-gurdy moans!
> In the basement nest the rats,
> Grog and beer on the ground floor
> And up to the fifth floor all the flats
> Hide suburban misery behind each door.*

---

* Translation of Arno Holz's *Ihr Dach stieß fast bis an die Sterne* (1898).

Inside a typical Berlin *Mietskaserne*. (© Deutsches Historisches
Museum, Berlin)

As the railway network in Germany was designed with industry in mind rather than as a means of increasing mobility and
connectivity for the wider population, there were excellent
connections between cities and from there to ports, rivers and
border points. However, it left the rural population stranded.
The inhabitants of German villages and hamlets continued to get around on foot or horseback, which limited their

geographical radius severely. Without telephone, radio, TV or the internet, newspapers were the only connection to the world beyond their immediate local area. The sense of being 'cut off' began to translate into 'left behind' very quickly and the resentment caused by this triggered a defensive and conservative backlash against the progress many in the cities were still so excited about. A deep suspicion arose in the countryside towards modernity and those 'clever folks' in the cities. The awesome spectacle of a steam train pulling out of a station, carrying its passengers hundreds of miles away in comfort, could only inspire enthusiasm in those who had access to it. The rest learnt to resent the world this technology stood for and how it devalued their way of life.

However, there was also a conservative backlash in other social and geographical spheres. This had begun with the 1873 crisis of capitalism, which had a peculiar effect on the middle classes. On the whole, many people who fell into this broad spectrum, from teachers and small business owners to powerful industrialists, had been enthusiastic supporters of the liberal movement that had helped bring about the unification of Germany. But the re-evaluation of capitalism after 1873 had led to a confidence crisis. A certain snobbery from the old elites towards the nouveaux riches began to grind its way into the minds of the middle classes. A trend began to affect the mannerisms and lifestyle of military and aristocratic elites. Where in 1871, a businessman would still proudly have worn a tailored suit on his wedding day, he would now try to buy an honorary army office or join a reserve unit, so that he could marry in uniform. Similarly, furniture, hairstyles and customs were beginning to ape those of the aristocracy. Those with enough money and influence would try to buy titles or marry into the nobility in order to add the much desired 'von' to their names. This was caused as much by the conservative shift in the 1880s as it was by a longing to return to better times. Now insecure about their recently acquired status and wealth, those who would have told the elites that their time was up in 1871, now looked to the long pedigree of noble families and envied it. It was a dangerous trend when combined with the Prussian legacy of militarism and a desire to hold on to the supposedly German values of loyalty and strength.

This overall conservative direction applied to women from all social strata as well. It is true that fashion became somewhat more relaxed, and the traditional long dresses were often replaced with a more practical combination of (long) skirts and blouses or shirts. But overall women still expected to get married and then support their husbands from home by looking after their children, house and hearth. As women could not attend universities until 1891, most middle-class professions were inaccessible to them. The only exception was teaching, which was considered an acceptable female vocation but only up until marriage. Bigger changes were seen in the ranks of working-class women. In the pre-industrial age, women were required to help out on farms, mending tools and equipment, contributing to the harvest and tending to livestock. Early industrialisation still meant that many women worked from home, often producing cloth and thus subsidising their husbands' incomes. The 1870s and '80s saw more and more working-class women working outside the home. This change was slow, by 1882 only around 500,000 women worked in factories, as there was still a stigma attached to the inability of men to provide enough for their families so that their wives could stay at home and look after the children. Women mostly still worked in low-skilled, monotonous factory jobs that earned them only 60 per cent of the wages of male workers, but campaigning had seen some improvement in the legislation around their working conditions. There was provision for maternity leave, working hours were capped, and night-working and hard labour were banned for women.

Much has recently been made of the early women's movement that began to organise itself from the mid-1860s. However, it is worth reminding ourselves that this was a tiny group of mostly bourgeois background who claimed to speak for all female factory workers. This often went hand in hand with other political causes. Women like Clara Zetkin, who was a schoolteacher and the partner of a Russian revolutionary, were hardly representative of this group who primarily worked not in the interest of female emancipation but in order to feed their children and keep a roof over their heads. Early feminists like Zetkin exemplify the dense intertwining of some elements of the female workers' movement with international socialism in the period. Other organisations such as the General German Women's Association (ADF) were middle class in origin and outlook, fighting for the right of women to enter the professions, go to university and gain equality in law. They ruled out working together with radical female socialists. Neither side represented the majority of German women who, on the whole, still saw their role in traditional terms. They wanted to be good mothers to their children and wives to their husbands, and thus often had as much disdain for the demands of women's organisations as their male contemporaries. There would only be a significant shift in this culture just before, during and after the First World War when there would emerge mass protests for women's rights, suffrage and equality.

The question, What is German? was also difficult to answer regarding the many national and religious minorities in the Reich. As Neil MacGregor has shown, being a continental power with few distinct physical boundaries made Germany culturally difficult to define. Linguistic fault lines did not always overlap with geographical or political ones. Millions of Polish,

Danish and French citizens ended up as national minorities within the boundaries of the German Empire in 1871. Their secession demands posed a real danger to the structural integrity of the new state. Bismarck recognised this threat and was quick to identify more *Reichsfeinde*, who were best dealt with by a process of 'negative integration', as he put it. This meant that over time, they should be forced, coerced and incentivised to become German in culture and language, if not in this generation, then in the next. To this end, Bismarck made German the only official language in schools, courtrooms and public life. This was enforced by local government which frequently inspected Polish schools in particular, where the rule was often deliberately defied in order to preserve the Polish culture that was threatened on both sides of the German–Russian border. State loans for land in East Prussia were designed to encourage Germans to move to heavily Polish-populated areas and thus 'dilute' the linguistic and cultural composition there. Also, schools, compulsory military service and universities deliberately created mixed groups and formations to encourage the melting of foreign cultures into the German pot. Danish calls for secession were simply ignored as the Danes in Holstein were too small a minority, and their culture and language deemed so similar to German that integration would just happen organically over time.

The French in the annexed territories of Alsace and Lorraine, on the other hand, were difficult to deal with and local outbreaks of resistance commonplace. Using his usual tactics of carrot and stick, Bismarck attempted to pacify the region by allowing it fifteen deputies in the Reichstag but no representation in the Bundesrat (the upper chamber that acted as a bulwark for state rights). Furthermore, he appointed governors for Alsace-Lorraine who were sympathetic to the federal government. In addition, Bismarck promoted Strasbourg University to incentivise people to stay, at the same time allowing those who wanted to leave to move to France, which 400,000 people would do by 1914. Secessionist Poles were treated with more contempt. Frustrated with the resistance in the Reichstag to expelling Poles, the Prussian state authorities took matters into their own hands in 1885 by expelling 35,000 Poles without German citizenship to Austria and Russia. Bismarck's role in this has been the subject of much debate. He was publicly critical of the measures but did not issue any punishments or even an official rebuke to the Prussian state authorities. These blunt and insensitive attempts to Germanise the population were crude and unnecessary. Compulsory military service, common schools and regular intermixing of the national minorities were forces of assimilation at work with or without 'negative integration'. Those with an intense hostility towards the German state, particularly French and Polish people, reacted naturally with even more resentment when exposed to insensitive integration measures.

The so-called 'Jewish Question' was a matter of considerable debate in the context of German nationhood. There were 512,000 Jews in Germany in 1871, and arguments about their emancipation had raged for some time even before unification. Both Bismarck and Kaiser Wilhelm saw Judaism as a religious issue rather than a racial one and argued that Jews should have full equality in law and even be allowed to take public offices and army positions so long as they were well integrated and ideally invisible as a minority. Jews were, therefore, encouraged to convert to Christianity, which 15,000 did in order to gain access to higher office. The agitation against Jews sharpened with the financial crash of 1873 when the usual tropes of the Jewish banker fuelled the anger about the economic situation. Another wave of anti-Semitism hit in the 1880s, when many Russian and Polish Jews fled to Germany after pogroms in the east. These new arrivals did not speak any German, were poorly educated and possessed few professional skills. Settling mainly in Prussia and Berlin specifically, they caused fears of undercutting the wages of semi-skilled German labour at a time of economic crisis. Bismarck frequently toned down the language of his conservative and Catholic allies in the Reichstag but equally did not deem the issue important enough to spend political capital on it. The deportation of Poles in 1885 also included 4,000 Jewish people, and as we have seen, Bismarck looked the other way when they were forcefully evicted from their homes and pushed into countries where pogroms and other forms of anti-Semitic violence were commonplace. However, the numbers of Jews in Germany would grow to 615,000 by 1910 and education, military service and general cultural assimilation meant that the vast majority lived side-by-side with their Christian compatriots in Bismarck's Reich.

Despite the division, suspicion and cultural insecurity, German society was still growing together gradually between 1871 and 1890. The compulsory military service of two years at a formative age had a transformative impact on a very young population. It created a sense of national belonging in men regardless of class, religious affiliation or political views that would last a lifetime and spill over into the next generation. Slowly a society emerged that shared values such as hard work, punctuality, honesty and precision, which became seen as intrinsically German. Despite the fault lines of class, age, gender, religion and national identity, at the end of Bismarck's reign, we see a mostly conservative population that valued order, prosperity and the national union he had built. But it was also one whose patriotic fervour needed a constant diet of conflict to fill the holes torn into the social fabric by inequality, geographical separation and cultural differences.

The Social Question: Bismarck and the Working Classes

The unbridled capitalism of the Second Industrial Revolution produced immense growth and an overall increase in living standards. But it also led to a debate about the fairness of how the new wealth was distributed among those who produced it. The rapid population growth combined with the processes of urbanisation and mechanisation had led to a swelling of the ranks of the proletariat. In the course of the nineteenth century, Karl Marx and others had rediscovered this term, which was used in Ancient Rome to describe a class of people who did not own land and were dependent on wages while remaining free to sell their labour. In the context of the Industrial Revolution, this was applied to the phenomenon of urban workers who used material, machinery and other means of production that they did not own to produce goods for a fixed wage. In contrast to a traditional weaver who owned his own loom, bought the wool and then used both to make cloth, which he then sold on the market for his own profit, the urban equivalent was a worker in a cloth factory where mechanical looms and wool were supplied, and the final product was sold on by others. Marx argued that this disenfranchised workers from their labour as what they earned stood in little or no relation to the profits that they had produced with their work. In the eyes of early socialists, the capitalists who owned the means of production held all the cards. All the while factory owners dealt with individual labourers, they could dictate wages and conditions, especially in an age where the division of labour and mechanisation had created many jobs that needed little or no training. Low-skilled workers had become replaceable commodities who could be pitted against each other. Early socialists argued that the only way to combat this trend was to organise and unite.

In the context of the liberal and socialist revolutions of 1848, Marx's opening lines to his communist manifesto sounded ominous: 'A spectre is haunting Europe — the spectre of communism. All the powers of old Europe have entered into a holy alliance to exorcise this spectre [...] Communism is already acknowledged by all European powers to be itself a power.'* But in 1871, the spectre did not loom quite so large any more. Working-class Germans were cheering for the unity of the fatherland, Bismarck and Wilhelm were heroes to many. The economic future was looking bright. Working-class parties had been formed in the North German Confederation: the Social Democratic Workers' Party (SDAP) in 1869 by Wilhelm Liebknecht and August Bebel and the General German Workers' Association (ADAV) in 1863 by Ferdinand Lassalle. But between them, they only received 3.2 per cent of the vote in the elections of March 1871, which amounted to two seats in the Reichstag. As we have already seen, Bismarck monitored the situation closely and met with Lassalle several times to frighten the liberals. Still, on the whole, he rightly judged that there was no communist spectre and that there were bigger obstacles in the way to stabilising the newly formed German Empire.

Besides, many Germans, including many workers, regarded the socialists as extremists and traitors. The term *vaterlandslose Gesellen* (literally: fellows without fatherland) had been used since the 1850s to discredit early socialists as disloyal and subversive. The claim that they had no allegiance to their country and were instead internationalists was particularly powerful in the context of the nationalist undercurrents in

---

*   Marx.

mid-nineteenth-century Europe. They had declared their sympathies for the French Republic that had emerged after Napoleon III's fall in 1870, and some had openly opposed the annexation of Alsace and Lorraine. There was even vocal support for the infamous and radical Paris Commune, a brief phase of revolutionary control of Paris in the spring of 1871. The violent regime there had killed two French army generals and set up a temporary dictatorship in the city that was criticised even by ardent supporters of the movement. While Marx began to justify the necessity of a 'Dictatorship of the Proletariat' to defend revolutions from reactionary suppression, in the eyes of many ordinary Germans this was an abhorrent example of political excess, and anyone who would side with such extremism over a united, monarchical Germany found little sympathy. Bismarck thus found it easy to brand this group too as *Reichsfeinde*.

However, the movement began to gain traction as the long depression of the 1870s began to affect working conditions. More and more labourers found themselves trapped in monotonous urban labyrinths where they toiled for over twelve hours a day often seven days a week, as their wives and children often also had to work to make ends meet. The situation became unbearable. Unemployment without social security meant starvation and homelessness, and so many were forced to work under whatever conditions their employers imposed, even when sick or injured. The need for workers to organise and fight for their interests now became an urgent necessity rather than a political ideology, and so many began to join the movement. This led to the merger of the SDAP and ADAV parties in 1875. Later renamed as the SPD, the Social Democratic Party of Germany is still one of the largest political parties in Germany today. While some of the leaders preached class warfare and called members to arms, many simply wanted social reform to help improve the lot of the urban working classes.

When August Bebel and Wilhelm Liebknecht were put on trial in 1872 for treason and both received two-year prison sentences, many felt that was no more than they deserved for their disloyalty to the fatherland. The authorities thus had got away with locking up two leading figures of the movement. But Bismarck sensed that since 1873 the mood had changed and trying to quell working-class anger with repression alone would not do. In the 1877 Reichstag elections, votes for the SPD had already risen to 9.1 per cent or 500,000 votes, which translated to twelve seats. Bismarck had tried to pass repressive measures that would make organisation, publication and funding more difficult for socialist groups, but he had found it impossible to convince the Reichstag to pass such legislation. Still working with the National Liberals, no cajoling, threats or backroom deals would be enough to convince them to pass gagging laws. Not only was the freedom of expression one of their core policies, but they suspected Bismarck might use such legislation against the liberal cause when it suited him. All of this played out very publicly in the press and Bismarck was waiting for a turn of public opinion that would help him pressurise the Reichstag into passing the legislation.

The opportunity would come in the spring of 1878. On 11 May, the 81-year-old Kaiser Wilhelm and his daughter Princess Louise were being driven up the magnificent Unter den Linden boulevard in central Berlin to wave to their cheering subjects. Suddenly, a man ran onto the road and pointed his revolver at the royals. He fired two shots before he was wrestled to the ground. In the commotion, one of the witnesses who had tried to help was severely injured and would die a few days later. Wilhelm himself and Princess Louise remained unharmed as both bullets had missed, but the incident gravely shook them. So it did the German public. The assassin was a plumber named Emil Max Hödel who had been a member of the Social Democratic Association in Leipzig until he was expelled for his anarchist views. His trial caused an outpouring of sympathy towards the old Kaiser, and Hödel was found guilty and executed in August of the same year. Despite having been expelled from the party, Hödel's association with the SPD would surely be enough to force the anti-socialist laws through the Reichstag, or so Bismarck thought. When he reintroduced the drafts, the National Liberals once more turned them down, arguing that one lone-wolf assassin did not justify the oppression of basic freedoms.

Bismarck would get another chance. Just a week after the defeat in the Reichstag, on 2 June 1878, a defiant Wilhelm was out again on Unter den Linden to the cheers of his people. Unbeknownst to him, a Dr Karl Nobiling had positioned himself in an apartment along the street with a double-barrelled shotgun. When the Kaiser passed underneath the window, Nobiling fired at him, with several grains hitting the old man in the chest and lower body. The assassin immediately shot himself with a revolver, later dying from the wound, while Wilhelm was rushed back to the palace, gravely injured. According to Bismarck's secretary Tiedemann, the chancellor reacted to the news that his Kaiser had been shot by throwing his walking stick on the ground and exclaiming, 'Now we will dissolve the Reichstag!' Only then did it occur to him to inquire about Wilhelm's health.* In his typical realpolitik style, Bismarck's first concern was how he could use the situation to win his battle with the Reichstag. The Kaiser survived; he had been saved by

---

*   Eyck.

his *Pickelhaube* helmet, which had protected his head from the shotgun's spray.

Nobiling had even more tenuous links to the SPD than Hödel but the fact that this time the Kaiser had actually been wounded was enough. Bismarck dissolved the Reichstag and called new elections. He claimed that the liberals had failed to protect Wilhelm by rejecting the anti-socialist bill and were thus practically complicit in the nefarious second assassination attempt. The German public rallied to defend their monarch and voted accordingly. The SPD lost nearly 200,000 votes, and by association, the National Liberals also lost 130,000 or twenty-nine seats. Not wanting to lose even more public footing, most of the remaining liberals now voted for the bill, as did the conservative parties, and it was passed in October 1878.

The so-called *Sozialistengesetze* banned all socialist organisations, including trade unions, public meetings and publications. They led to the arrest of 1,500 socialists, while many others fled abroad. But socialism and social reform were movements in Europe that could not be halted by legislation. While the SPD was banned as a party, there was nothing to stop individual candidates from standing as independents and thus some socialists, such as founding members Wilhelm Liebknecht and August Bebel, were elected into the Reichstag, where they could speak freely. When the anti-socialist laws were eventually lifted in 1890, the SPD gained over a million votes and thirty-five seats in the Reichstag. They would swell further and become the single largest party in the German parliament by 1912.

Bismarck recognised that he could not stem the tide, and so he quickly sought to bring the working classes on side through his policy of 'state socialism'. The carrot to the stick of repressive legislation, this consisted of a series of progressive measures to pacify the working class enough to take the political anger out of them. Even the staunchest supporters of the old system agreed that the so-called 'social question' needed to be addressed, and as such, there was little resistance when Bismarck introduced his welfare measures. In 1883, he passed a Sickness Insurance Act, which provided up to thirteen weeks of sick pay. The Accident Insurance Act followed in 1884, solely funded by employers, and thus gave excellent reasons for improving health and safety conditions in workplaces. Perhaps the most revolutionary measure was the 1889 Old Age and Disability Act, which gave pensions to people over 70 and those who could not work.

While often described as a shameful bribe to make up for the repressive anti-socialist laws, Bismarck's policies must be seen in the context of the time. He overreacted to a social-ist threat that had not yet materialised. Equally, he created one of the most substantial and progressive welfare states of his time. Perhaps he did so as a realpolitik measure in order to keep workers quiet, discredit the liberals and gain con-servative support. Still, if that was what it took to establish the foundations of a welfare state in the supposedly most regres-sive political system in Europe, then it is understandable why many workers continued to support the existing social and political order.

Foreign Policy

In the famous *Kissingen Dictation* of 1877, in which Otto von Bismarck laid out the principles of his foreign policy, he tellingly spoke of a '*cauchemar des coalitions*' – a nightmare of coa-litions – the fear of which underpinned everything. Right from the outset, the creation of a German Empire in the heart of continental Europe bore the risk of uniting the surrounding powers into an opposing coalition that would at best limit the scope of Germany's ability to act and at worst destroy it. Bismarck was therefore at pains to stress that German territorial ambitions were 'saturated' and that the settling of the German Question would not mean a major reshuffle of European power relations. However, Bismarck was also realistic enough to understand that France would not be won over easily. The annexation of Alsace and Lorraine had cemented the 'hereditary' enmity between both states and thus perpetuated this particular conflict into the foreseeable future. Bismarck's aim was, therefore, to look eastwards for support and isolate the French threat. As early as 1863, he had remarked, 'The secret of politics? Make a good treaty with Russia.'

With France in economic and political turmoil after the 1870 war with Prussia, the window of opportunity was there. Napoleon III was gone, and the French Republic made an unpalatable ally to Russia and Austria, which wished to hold on to their monarchies and the old system. The parallels between 1870 and the French defeat in 1815 did not escape the politically astute Bismarck, and he was quick to remind his Austrian and Russian counterparts of the so-called 'Holy Alliance' they had formed with Prussia in 1815. A revival of sorts was agreed in 1873 in the *Dreikaiserbund*, the Union of the Three Emperors, between the Tsar and the two Kaisers of Germany and Austria-Hungary. Mainly concerned with controlling Eastern Europe and the Balkans, it nonetheless isolated the French to a point where they felt so threatened that they launched a massive rearmament programme after the last German troops had left the country in 1873. Ever the scheming realpolitiker, Bismarck provoked the so-called 'war-in-sight' crisis in 1875 in order to counter French sabre-rattling before it had even begun. Almost certainly penned by Bismarck, a series of articles appeared in the pro-government *Berliner Post* that publicly speculated about a pre-emptive war against France. At the same time, Bismarck had stopped the export of horses and other war-related goods to France, creating the illusion of imminent war. The upshot was that France asked Russia and Britain for support and received public reassurance from both that they would not tolerate German aggression against France. As Bismarck describes in the *Kissingen Dictation*, this incident proved once and for all that there was absolutely no diplomatic room for Germany to expand beyond its current reaches. The night-mare of coalitions, and the attendant two-front war, would mean the destruction of the Reich and no expansion of ter-ritory was worth that risk. If only Wilhelm II had read and understood the old chancellor's words.

Bismarck dedicated the rest of his political life to creating a complicated network of alliances and reassurances, which would carve out a role for Germany as the 'honest broker'. When a Balkan crisis erupted in 1877–78 between Austria and Russia, with both seeking to extend their influence in this stra-tegically important region, Bismarck invited all the European powers to the Congress of Berlin and war was averted. For the first time, Berlin took centre stage in European power poli-tics, and it was in the role of the 'honest broker' as Bismarck had intended.

But as central as Russia was in Bismarck's appreciation, conflict with the Eurasian giant could not be avoided for long. The grain tariffs of 1879 had hit Russian exports particularly hard, and this was made worse by a ban on Russian meat due to a plague outbreak in the previous year.* Suspicions had already run high on the Russian side as there was an expectation that some of Germany's north-eastern territory in the Baltic region would be ceded to Russia in exchange for its neutrality during the unification process. Tsar Alexander II's temper flared in August 1879 when he wrote a letter to his uncle Kaiser Wilhelm I, which was so harsh in tone that it became known as the *Ohrfeigenbrief* – a letter akin to a slap in the face. The document blamed Bismarck in name for the deterioration of Russo-German relations. The Kaiser invited his nephew the Tsar to talks in order to smooth relations again. Meanwhile, Bismarck was busy hammering out a defensive agreement with Austria, known as the Dual Alliance, which became effective in October 1879. Russia stood by helplessly when Italy joined in 1882 and extended the treaty into a Triple Alliance. It is testament to Bismarck's diplomatic skill that he managed to bring Russia back to the table in a revival of the Three-Kaiser League in 1881 and its extension in 1884. When relations between Austria and Russia broke down irrevocably over the Balkans, Bismarck eventually resorted to cleverly managed bilateral agreements, most notably the Reinsurance Treaty with Russia 1887. In this top-secret treaty that thus avoided alienating France and Austria, Germany and Russia agreed to remain neutral should they be attacked by a third party. With the French War Minister Georges Boulanger talking openly about a war of revenge against Germany since 1886, this was just the kind of protective agreement that Germany needed to shield itself from the nightmare of coalitions.

When Wilhelm I died in 1888, he passed on a Germany that was tied into the European network of states in an intricate,

---

*   Heilbronner.

complicated and fragile net of Bismarck's making. Only the Iron Chancellor understood the carefully crafted secret and open ties that he had spun. Only he knew the diplomats and relevant authorities in each country well enough to play his diplomatic cards to perfection. The only question was, would the new Kaiser let him play?

3

THREE EMPERORS AND A CHANCELLOR 1888-90

'I have seen three emperors in their nakedness, and the sight was not inspiring ...'

Otto von Bismarck

1888: The Year of the Three Emperors

The longevity of Kaiser Wilhelm I had surprised many. Almost 74 years old when the German Empire was created in 1871, he had lived through its long and violent evolution and had become a national symbol of almost mythical proportions, if a somewhat unwilling one. Insiders at court expected him to lead the new state into its first few unified years before his son would take over the helm as Friedrich III. This caused optimism and dread respectively in the different factions of the political circles as the Crown Prince had long been openly critical of the conservative turn his father and Bismarck had taken. He had instead advocated a more liberal course that would seek parliamentary reform and closer relations with Britain rather than Russia. Friedrich's English wife, Victoria, who was Queen Victoria's eldest daughter, had also made many enemies at court. An intelligent, sharp-witted and outspoken woman, her demeanour and direct intervention in her husband's affairs seemed unseemly and manipulative to many in the conservative camp. As she was much stronger willed than her husband, rumours quickly spread that it was she who was driving Friedrich into opposing his father. As the German Kaiser got older, a certain anticipation developed in both political camps, with the liberals hoping for long-awaited change and the conservatives, such as Bismarck himself, dreading a political reshuffle.

As old Wilhelm lived on for year after year, a strange situation emerged. Not only was the heir asserting his own political will but so was the heir's son. Wilhelm II was in his twenties in the 1880s. While his grandfather was still in power and entirely capable of running state affairs together with Bismarck, the young prince began to use the situation to outmanoeuvre his parents. This would have been nigh-on impossible if Friedrich and Victoria had already reigned as king and queen. With young Wilhelm making it more and more obvious that he despised the liberalism of his mother and father and was more in line with his grandfather's conservative inclinations, it became increasingly difficult for the court to work out which of the two they needed to groom and please in order to retain political power into the future. It certainly would not be possible to keep both generations of Hohenzollern princes happy. As it turned out, the conundrum solved itself. On 12 November 1887, an official announcement made public that Friedrich had incurable cancer of the throat. Clearly he would not have long to live. It was a terrible blow to those who had set their hearts on a new liberal era of German politics, but the court now began to shift its attention wholly to young Wilhelm.

Bismarck's preparations to work with the young Hohenzollern took on a new sense of urgency. Through his son Herbert, the chancellor had long cultivated an almost fatherly relationship with the future Kaiser and he had shown him the ropes in the fields of diplomacy, court intrigue and politics. Nothing less than Bismarck's life work was at stake. War with Russia loomed large on the horizon and domestically his policy of 'saturation' came under fire with more and more powerful calls for German expansion and empire-building piling on the pressure. In addition, the socialist movement had grown, and strikes threatened to seriously disrupt the social fabric of the nation. With his grandfather nearing his 90s and his father ill with cancer, the young contender to the throne had to be carefully prepared for his role as king. Bismarck was quite open about the fact that he thought him a 'hothead [who] could not hold his tongue, was susceptible to flatterers, and was capable of plunging Germany into a war without knowing what he was doing'.* He might ruin everything and plunge Germany into the abyss with a careless slip of the tongue or one of his diplomatic blunders if left unchecked.

The old Kaiser died at the age of 90 on 9 March 1888 and his son took over as Friedrich III. The fact that the latter only reigned for ninety-nine days before succumbing to the cancer in his throat did not leave enough time for a change in personnel or policy at the court.† If Victoria held any hopes that her brief time as queen and her position as mother of the new Kaiser bought her any influence in German politics, she was mistaken. The relationship between her and Wilhelm had been complicated from birth. Still, the last few years before 1888 had culminated in such mutual distrust that Wilhelm wanted to publicly break with her. When Friedrich had first been told that he had cancer, Victoria would not believe that an opera-

---

* Quoted from Ullrich, p.104.
† Clark, *Wilhelm*, p.25.

tion was necessary and instead chose to trust her English doctor, who assured her that her husband would get better with rest. After Friedrich's death, Wilhelm had his body opened, and the pathologist found large amounts of cancerous tissue in his throat, proving that the illness had been advanced. Evidently Victoria had been wrong to advocate the nonsurgical course. This was quickly spun into another malicious yarn in the fabric of rumours that had long portrayed her as the scheming woman behind all of Friedrich's misguided actions. There would be no role for Victoria at Wilhelm's side when he became German Kaiser on 15 June 1888 at the age of 29.

1888–90: Two Men at the Helm

Wilhelm wholeheartedly agreed with Bismarck on the fact that the latter was indispensable. For now. 'I shall not manage without the chancellor at first, but in due course I hope [...] to be able to dispense with Prince Bismarck's cooperation.'* It was clear, however, that this was not the same emotional and political dependency that his grandfather had felt towards the *junker*. Where his grandfather had reluctantly agreed to German unity as a means of extending Prussian power, Wilhelm wanted to be a neo-absolutist Kaiser of all Germans. In his vision of himself as a reincarnation of the mythical Frederick Barbarossa who had come to lead the Germans back to greatness, there was no room for chancellors, ministers and political realities. With typical overconfidence in his own charisma, Wilhelm thought he was going to be loved, respected and if necessary feared by sheer force of his personality. He had no comprehension of the complicated Bismarckian foreign and domestic schemes that held

---

* Quoted from Clark, *Wilhelm*, p.24.

the German Empire together and had allowed it to prosper. It did not help that Bismarck's constitution was entirely designed around his own relationship with Wilhelm I. The necessary dependency of Kaiser and chancellor upon one another allowed for only one of the two to be dominant, while the other had to take a submissive role. A situation with two stubborn Prussians at the helm of the German ship did not bode well.

Young Wilhelm with Otto von Bismarck.

A serious rift between the monarch and his chancellor did not take long to emerge. With the socialist movement gaining traction on the ground in factories and on the streets, Bismarck planned to sharpen his anti-socialist laws further and extend them to be valid in perpetuity, effectively banning all social-ist activity. This would stoke the anger of the mass strikes further, making the old chancellor indispensable to Wilhelm, who would need an experienced hand to deal with the problem. When Bismarck introduced this draft to the Reichstag in October 1889, Wilhelm was concerned that this would get his reign off to a bad start. Knowing full well that even the debate of such laws would fuel demonstrations and strikes to a point where he might have to send in soldiers to put them down, he demanded that Bismarck tone down the language of the laws. In his Royal Decree of 4 February 1890, he told his chancellor that he was 'resolved to lend a hand in improving the situation of German workers'.* He wanted to be loved by his new subjects, and the way to achieve this was not with a bloody massacre of workers. Bismarck had got used to decades of Hohenzollern submission and so did not move an inch, expecting Wilhelm to give in. Instead, this was the opportunity the Reichstag had been waiting for. After years of Bismarckian domination, even former allies like Centre Party politician Peter Reichensperger now sensed that the *junker*'s time was up and they let his anti-socialist bill collapse. There was clearly no room for two strong heads at the top of a divided national body.

1890: Dropping the Pilot

When Bismarck eventually handed in his letter of resignation on 18 March 1890, it was after months of hesitation. The elections of 20 February returned an impossible parliamentary arithmetic. The SPD had gained an additional twenty-four seats, becoming the largest party in terms of the popular vote with 19.7 per cent, while the also reform-minded Centre Party remained dominant with 106 seats. The chancellor became so

---

* Kaiser Wilhelm II's Decree of 4 February 1890.

desperate to cling on to power that he resorted to drastic measures. As late as 2 March he was openly outlining the option of a complete overthrow of the constitution to the German nobility, suggesting that they could abandon the existing system and with it the rebellious Reichstag, instead ruling through joint decision making. When this plot was shot down, Bismarck tried to revive his conservative alliance with the Centre Party by approaching its leader, Ludwig Windthorst, on 12 March. He too refused, sensing that the old Prussian's political days were numbered and that real power now lay with Wilhelm II. Windthorst was also acutely aware of the proportion of strikers who were Catholic: he needed to represent their demands for reform if he was to hold on to the spectacular election results. The leader of the Centre Party could not and would not help an old man whose star was waning. This left Bismarck wedged between an extremely hostile Reichstag and a power-hungry Kaiser waiting for an opportunity to dismiss him.

The final straw came on the morning of 15 March 1890 when Bismarck woke up to the news that Wilhelm wanted to see him in the foreign office within the hour. The relatively small but elegant villa at Wilhelmstraße 76 was next door to the chancellor's flat in number 77. The two-storey building had always been cramped and rather too small for its purpose, but its position served Bismarck well in his double role as director of internal and external affairs of the Reich. When the old *junker* reported to his Kaiser, Wilhelm ended the power struggle there and then by emotionally withdrawing all support for Bismarck in front of his assembled inner circle of military and political advisors. The awkward scene proved to all and sundry that the old chancellor's time was up. Having lost the confidence of the monarch for all to see, Bismarck had no choice but to resign. The fact that it then took him two days to write his resignation letter shows just what a momentous occasion this was and how conscious the Iron Chancellor was of his image then and in posterity. A linguistic masterpiece even by Bismarck's standards, the elegant letter managed to shift the responsibility for Bismarck's resignation entirely over to Wilhelm:

> Considering my attachment to service for the monarchy and for Your Majesty and the long-established relationship which I had believed would exist forever, it is very painful for me to terminate my accustomed relationship to the All Highest and to the political life of the Reich and Prussia; [...] I would have submitted the request for dismissal from my offices to Your Majesty earlier, had I not been under the impression that it was Your Majesty's wish to make use of the experience and talents of a loyal servant to His ancestors. Now that I am certain that Your Majesty does not require these, I may withdraw from political life without fearing that my decision will be condemned as untimely by public opinion.*

Otto von Bismarck's resignation marked the beginning of a new era of personal rule by Wilhelm II. Germany had dropped its experienced pilot, and the 31-year-old Kaiser took the helm. Germany, Europe and the world looked on as an era came to an end and a new one began.

---

* Bismarck's Letter of Resignation (18 March 1890).

Sir John Tenniel's famous cartoon published in *Punch* magazine in
Britain, March 1890.

4

WILHELM'S REICH 1890-1914

'The kaiser is like a balloon: if you don't keep fast hold of the string, you never know where he will be off to.'

Otto von Bismarck

Personal Rule or Shadow Emperor?

'*Suprema lex regis voluntas*' – 'The will of the king is the highest law' – wrote Wilhelm II in 1891 into the Golden Book of the City of Munich. It is one of many self-aggrandising statements that sum up the young Kaiser's self-image as ruler perfectly. No longer would Germany be governed by an overbearing old bureaucrat like Bismarck, but a glorious new imperial era was to dawn that would inspire the German people to overcome their differences and find a national focal point in their Kaiser. This 'policy of consolidation and conciliation'* would become the hallmark of Wilhelm's early phase of kingship. However, the principles on which it relied were dangerous, not least among

---

★   Clark, *Wilhelm*, p.79.

them a hostility towards the supposed enemies to German greatness: socialists, democrats and foreign rivals. The young Kaiser built up a glittering facade of imperial pomp in his palaces and castles that deliberately contrasted with the frugal interior of the chancellery in the Wilhelmstrasse. He thus tried to create an image of monarchical power that seemed outdated, even anachronistic to many. By the turn of the century, it would begin to unravel.

The period from 1890 to 1914 has often been dubbed 'Wilhelmine' and for good reason. Just as Bismarck dominated the first phase of the German Empire from 1871 to 1890, Wilhelm put his own stamp on the period leading up to the First World War, at which point he was sidelined by the military establishment. It seems somewhat ironic that Bismarck had prided himself on protecting the German monarchy from the reduced status seen in other countries such as Britain, Italy or the Netherlands. There, constitutional ties had supposedly turned kings and queens into little more than 'automatic signing machines'.* Bismarck nevertheless decided to put himself, as chancellor, at the heart of the first German constitution. But Wilhelm had other plans. He wanted no chancellor, parliament or ministers to mitigate his power. As Hans-Ulrich Wehler put it, 'he tried to be both Chancellor and Emperor in one'.† That this was a wholly unworkable concept at the turn of the century only became apparent to Wilhelm when it was already too late. The contempt in which he held the constitution as a whole and the Reichstag in particular allowed powerful lobbies, personal advisors and political pressure groups to gain informal power unchecked by the constraints of a legal framework. Wilhelm

---

*   Röhl, p.41.
†   Wehler, p.62.

had neither the personality nor the political acumen to stand alone among the tumult of late nineteenth-century Europe.

While Bismarck spent his retirement writing bitter political commentary in sympathetic newspapers, Wilhelm stood isolated and inexperienced at the helm of a complex and powerful European nation that was on the brink of drastic changes both at home and abroad. With the tides of socialism and democratisation raging internally, external pressures such as the rapidly deteriorating relationship with Russia also loomed large. Wilhelm would need help, whether he liked it or not. As he had no regard for Bismarck's constitutional structures, he relied on a small group of personal advisors who began to gather around him, the so-called *camarilla*. His peculiar mix of swaggering overconfidence and obvious insecurity made it easy for flatterers and cunning manipulators to get through to the Kaiser and influence his decision making. A key example was Wilhelm's friend, Philipp zu Eulenburg. Twelve years his senior, the sophisticated and elegant count impressed the young Kaiser with his well-groomed appearance and polished manners. And he in turn took a shine to the young Hohenzollern. His mystical-romantic tendencies led him to compose music and poetry, some of which was dedicated to Wilhelm, thus playing perfectly into the Kaiser's overstated self-image. Both shared an idealised vision of kingship that they sought to implement, and their friendship deepened to such a level that Eulenburg was allowed to address Wilhelm with the informal second-person pronoun *du*. Thanks to the Kaiser's favour, he was able to take on various positions as Prussian envoy and eventually even managed to start building his own power base, getting friends and relatives appointed into key offices, such as his cousins August and Botho to Marshall of the Court and Minister of the Interior respectively. This intimate clique of advisors eventually also included Bernard von Bülow (who would later become chancellor) and Count von Moltke. It was a closed circle with immense power over the Kaiser that would be despised by republicans and liberals for the 'uncoordinated authoritarianism'* it allowed to develop.

However, despite all his faults, the Kaiser caught the imagination of his people. His energetic and confident demeanour seemed to usher in a fresh start from the stagnation and stalemate under the old Bismarckian regime. The youthful and impulsive monarch seemed to embody the rapid changes the German economy and society were undergoing in the 1890s, and this was welcomed by many. With his keen, almost childlike, interest in modern technology, from steam engines to shipbuilding, the Kaiser also believed that Germany's leading role in innovation was good for public morale and nationbuilding. He promoted many scientific projects and patronised the foundation of institutions such as the Kaiser Wilhelm Society, which was founded in 1911 and is now known as the Max Planck Society. He also hosted one of the first auto races, an early version of the German Grand Prix, in 1907, which was named the *Kaiserpreis* in his honour. His personal enthusiasm for all things modern was well known among the German public as he travelled around the country visiting factories, ports and universities. In fact, he rarely ever seemed to stand still. On average spending less than 100 days a year in Berlin, he became known as the *Reisekaiser* – the travelling emperor. He thus posed a deliberate counter-image to his grandfather who, despite the odd public display, preferred a more withdrawn life and remained largely in Prussia where he felt at home. Where Wilhelm I had been old, modest and Prussian, Wilhelm II was young, audacious and German.

---

*   Ibid.

It is interesting that the recent debate around Kaiser Wilhelm's personality has largely been dominated by John Röhl and Christopher Clark – one a British, the other an Australian historian. Few German scholars have approached the subject outright. Röhl has rightly pointed out that there is something almost 'traumatic' about the way that Germans have omitted Wilhelm from their historical narrative. He describes how the last German Kaiser had become an 'Unperson'* since the end of the Second World War, while the British have retained a seemingly never-ending fascination with his grandmother, Victoria. Assertions about Wilhelm's biography and his character must, therefore, be taken with some caution. It would be a fallacy to see in Wilhelm's every fault a glint of pathology and madness that inevitably led to the outbreak of the First World War and subsequent conflict. Still, there is no doubt that he was a child of his time and that the militarism, nationalism and insecurity of the Germany he grew up in left a strong mark on his young mind.

Much has been made of Wilhelm's disability and the impact this had on his political outlook. His birth had been a difficult one. Keen to avoid a Caesarean section, the doctor had yanked Wilhelm out of his mother's womb, damaging nerves in the baby's shoulder in the process. This meant the young prince could not move his left arm, and it remained withered and useless for the rest of his life. Wilhelm saw himself as the embodiment of his nation, and a disability was thus an enormous blot on the image he sought to portray of Germany. He, therefore, hid the arm well, usually behind his back and in a glove. He learnt how to eat, ride and even shoot just with his one good arm. Nonetheless, the blemish remained a source of insecurity for the rest of his life. It is difficult to gauge to what

---

*   In Klussmann, p.94.

extent this affected his policymaking. It goes too far to suggest that Wilhelm's naval programme and blunderous foreign policy can all be traced back to the supposed childhood trauma. Undoubtedly, however, the disability would have fed into a deep-seated insecurity that manifested itself in his love for all things military, masculine and brash.

Wilhelm's love–hate relationship with England is a somewhat more traceable factor in his actions. Due to his close connection with the British royal family, he spent much of his childhood in England fascinated with its empire, naval power and aristocratic culture. From his grandmother Queen Victoria's favourite residence of Osborne House on the Isle of Wight, the young prince could overlook the Solent and watch the glorious fleet of the British navy sail in and out of Portsmouth and Southampton. Fascinated, Wilhelm became a keen boatsman himself, taking part in competitions and even hosting his own Emperor's Cup in 1904. As a boy, Wilhelm had confided to his uncle, the Prince of Wales, that he was hoping to have 'a fleet of my own someday'. After a poor showing on the German side at Queen Victoria's Fleet Review in 1889, Wilhelm resolved to build a navy that would be the envy of the world. He also loved the style of the English aristocracy and would often dress up to look like them. During the First World War, he had the Cecilienhof in Potsdam built in the style of a Tudor country manor. This odd fascination and rivalry with Britain meant that Wilhelm looked to the European neighbour as both a model for what he wanted to achieve with Germany and a competitor that had to be bested. It was yet another example of his childlike outlook on the world that would become a dangerous vehicle for the expansionists and warmongers in his inner circle at court.

It is tempting to dismiss Wilhelm's role from 1890 to 1914 as that of a 'shadow emperor' whose infantile disposition made it easy for others to manipulate him. While the victors in 1918 decided that responsibility for the First World War lay squarely with the Kaiser (his abdication was a non-negotiable precondition for peace), later generations have seen this differently. The aftermath of the Second World War began a reversal in the assessment of Wilhelm's ability to make decisions. Keen to find meaningful connections between both world wars, historians made the forces of Prussian, militaristic court culture the narrative link. After all, Wilhelm could hardly be blamed directly for the heinous crimes committed under Hitler's regime. This view has led to Wilhelm's figure receding in German collective memory. He became an eccentric and misguided tool for those who really held the strings of power. This narrative is oversimplifying the matter and lets Wilhelm off too lightly. When he ascended to the throne in 1890, he had a clear vision for Germany. He wanted a unified nation with a strong central monarchy that was world-leading in terms of technological, military and naval power. To this end, he chose to pay no heed to Bismarck's warnings about the precarious foreign policy situation, nor to the demands of the workers on the streets and in the factories. While it would be false to assume that Wilhelm led a massive rearmament programme and followed an imperialist policy in order to provoke a major European war, it is certainly true that he chose this path accepting that it might.

Imperial Germany as an Economic Powerhouse

Between the high grey stone facades that frame the long, wide avenues all the way to the horizon, an electric tram trundles past. Underground a U-Bahn train rattles towards Potsdamer Platz. In his chauffeur-driven Benz sits a young Walther Rathenau staring at Old Berlin – 'the palace with its

Berlin, *c*.1900.

ever-cursed chapel, the ungainly Neue Wache and Altes Museum'.[*] Berlin exemplifies the rapid changes of the times like no other German place. Only a few years earlier, Edison's electrical light had still been a marvel to behold. 'At Chausseestrasse young Walther had flicked the invention's switch off and on, filled with wonder until his father pushed him away, knocking him to the ground, telling him it wasn't a toy.'[†] By 1899, Rathenau had joined the AEG board. Germany's biggest electrical company had, only four years earlier, built Berlin's first underground train connection and would grow to dominate the electrical market together with its rival, Siemens. The Kaiser was fascinated by it all and invited Rathenau and others like him to the palace to discuss the modern marvels of technology and patronise further research and development. Like Germany

---

[*]   MacLean, p.89.
[†]   Ibid., p.88.

itself, Berlin was in transition. Horse-drawn carriages could be seen alongside electrified trams. Old neo-romantic facades were just a short walk away from glittering department stores like the famous *Kaufhaus des Westens* (KaDeWe), which in turn contrasted with the dreary workers' districts and their rows and rows of grey apartment blocks. Berlin would swell to 2 million inhabitants by 1905 and be catapulted from sleepy 'Prussian garrison town to metropolis'[*] with bewildering speed. On the one hand, this created immense excitement and a flurry of scientific and technological activity. Combustion engines, electricity and medical advances had all grown out of their infancy in the 1870s and '80s and broken through the barrier of practicability into widespread application. Leading physicists such as Max Planck worked in Berlin and were involved with the Kaiser Wilhelm Society. This, in turn, attracted further world-class scientists to the German capital, most notably Albert Einstein, who had been born in Ulm, Württemberg. With such high-calibre research and powerful financial backing, Germany's new industries 'pulled the German economy into a whirlwind boom period after March 1895', as Hans-Ulrich Wehler has comprehensively shown in his meticulous economic study of the German Empire.[†]

The economic and political misery that the German people had to live through with little respite from the First World War well into the 1950s may have led to a rather rose-tinted viewing of the supposed prosperity of the Kaiserreich.[‡] But despite the uneven nature of growth in geographical, chronological and structural terms, overall the German economy experienced a period of massive growth that was perceived as a boom by contemporaries, too. From the already accelerated levels of

---

[*]   Wassermann.
[†]   Wehler, p.42.
[‡]   Ullrich, p.127.

the Bismarckian era, German industrial production increased again by an incredible third in the years 1895–1900 alone. Reinvestment of profits into production and development was high and the total value added of the German economy had risen by 75 per cent by 1913. With a limited German market for this vast output, external markets were explored, and exports went through the roof, increasing from 2.9 billion marks in 1880 to 10.1 billion in 1913. Just before the First World War, the value of goods passing through the port of Hamburg was the third highest in the world, surpassed only by Antwerp and New York. German shipbuilding too had grown immensely, not in small part due to Wilhelm's personal love for all things nautical, and it accounted for one-tenth of world production. Germany had become an economic powerhouse that began to rival the biggest in the world. This gave the German people and their Kaiser a sense of national confidence in light of which old Bismarck's warnings about foreign political caution seemed a relic of a time gone by.

However, the impression of rapid progress is only one part of the picture. With specific new industries shooting ahead into a prosperous future, many other sectors of the German economy were left behind and fell into repeated cycles of depression and boom, with the recessions of 1901 and 1907 hitting particularly hard. This, in turn, created a constant undercurrent of anti-capitalist sentiment and economic anxiety among sections of the population. Marx had already predicted years earlier that the insatiable need for profit in industrialised nations would lead to structural economic problems, and at the turn of the century, many believed that he was right. The rapid population growth from 41 million in 1871 to 65 million in 1910 combined with the increasing mechanising in production lines that made unskilled labour a mass phenomenon meant that supply of work was a commodity that could be turned on and off by

industrialists as needed. In periods when production had overshot saturation point, mass unemployment awaited and hit the
now urbanised population of wage workers the hardest. The first
serious wave of this occurred in the wake of the 1907 depression, which made 319,000 people unemployed. But another
spike even surpassed this in 1913 with a figure of 348,000.
Wages too were out of step with the pace of the economic
growth overall. Where comparable Western economies saw an
average rise in real wages of approximately 4 per cent between
1890 and 1914, Germany's only rose by 1 per cent. Where did
the accumulated wealth go? One answer is the so-called 'invisible sector' of financial services, which directed immense profits
into the hands of a new elite of investors. Germany became
the world's third-largest creditor nation, and internally German
banks controlled much of the cash flow, centralising it into
large syndicates rather than small businesses. From this, a long
history of suspicion against bankers and the financial elites
emerged, which intertwined conveniently with the constant
undercurrents of anti-Semitism. Wealthy Jewish industrialists
and investors such as Walther Rathenau were quick to openly
embrace German traditions, convert to Christianity and affect
the mannerisms and style of the old aristocracy. Still, they could
never quite shake off the suspicion and hostility of those disaffected with this new style of free-flowing capitalism.

Another side-effect of the relatively unregulated market
was the rise of 'corporate capitalism' that Wehler has so thor-
oughly investigated in his work.* The 'invisible hand' of market
forces as described by Adam Smith and other forefathers of
capitalist theory seemed tied down in the eyes of many wage
workers, who began to feel an increasing squeeze on their
wages and living conditions caused by the monopolisation and

---

*   Wehler, Ch. II.

cartelisation of the economy. Where factories and companies in the same branch of industry merged or made agreements, wages and prices could be controlled, profit margins protected and competition for workers decreased. This left employees with very little leverage when negotiating for working hours, salaries or conditions. The desire for a similar degree of coordination on their side led to increased trade union membership – figures stood at an incredible 3 million in 1913 – and increasing politicisation of this social class. The SPD became the single largest party in the Reichstag in 1912 and thus posed a serious source of opposition on the eve of the First World War.

Agriculture was another sector weighed by pessimism. While two-thirds of Germans still lived in communities of under 2,000 inhabitants in 1871, the figure was as low as 40 per cent by 1910. The rural population had become an underappreciated minority. While new fertilisers, mechanisation and agricultural research had led to a massive jump in production, it also led to a slump in prices. They had fallen by 20 per cent by 1890, making the average farmer poorer rather than wealthier as was the case in every other sector of the economy. This was partially a structural problem, the effects of which we can still see in modern economies today. The mass production of food inevitably leads to low prices, and profit margins in agriculture get squeezed to unsustainable levels as this sector becomes less and less viable. But an additional problem in Germany was the fact that the aristocratic elites, and Prussian *junkers* in particular, resisted cultural change. Seeing land ownership and their way of life as a tradition that had to be conserved and protected against the unpalatable 'greed culture' of the nouveaux riches, modern economic management techniques, innovation and investment were not on the table. This left the agricultural sector stuck in limbo between feudal traditions and mass production – a fatal combination that drove much of its workforce into the cities.

Wilhelm's regime also did little to connect rural communities to the bustling cities. Cut off, underappreciated and increasingly squeezed by poverty, resentment grew, and cultural rifts widened. Organisations such as the German Agrarian League, which had grown to 330,000 members by 1913, spoke powerfully for their aristocratic members while agricultural labourers and small farmers suffered in resentful silence.

Under the leadership of its brash young Kaiser, an increasingly confident nation began to look for economic opportunities beyond the boundaries set by Bismarck's foreign policy. The clamour for economic expansionism began to grow from the circles of both old and new elites. Where the *junkers* needed export markets to solve the problem of agricultural overproduction, industrialists feared that Germany would eventually outgrow its supply of raw materials. Both groups pointed to Britain and France and their world-spanning empires and argued that Germany would never be able to compete in the long run unless it built an economic empire for itself. They formed powerful pressure groups such as the Pan-German League, which heavily leant on theories of Social Darwinism whereby Germany would have to struggle for its place in Europe. Thus empire-building became a question of national survival. Not the largest of the pressure groups, the Pan-German League nevertheless had influential members, 'well endowed with money and media influence'[*] and was thus able to influence public opinion. It worked in close cooperation with the German Colonial Society, which had 42,000 members by 1914. Among these were several members of parliament, whom it sponsored. Playing directly into Wilhelm's own fantasies and desire to rival Britain, both groups could now add economic arguments to their persuasive arsenal.

---

[*]   Sturmer, Ch. 4.

The years from 1890 to 1914 saw a confident nation emerge with a powerful economic backbone that drove the clamour for expansion. Where Bismarck had urged caution and had stressed that Germany's ambitions, financial or otherwise, were limited to central Europe, Wilhelm lifted the lid on this and let out nationalist calls for worldwide expansion. From the outset, this had an ugly undercurrent of Social Darwinism about it that made the other European powers nervous. Where there was talk of Germany's struggle to assert itself and find its rightful place among the nations of the world, the concept of the balance of powers suddenly faded into the background. Outnumbering Britain and France in output of steel, coal, industrial production and population, Germany had all the ingredients for war by 1914 and no good strategic reason to shy away from conflict if anyone dared stand in the way of the young nation's path to greatness. In addition, the continued technological and economic success had proved to be a powerful source of national pride that inspired a patriotic unity in many Germans regardless of all their differences. The appeal of 'social imperialism' was great.

A New Course: Leo Von Caprivi 1890–94

Having received Bismarck's resignation letter on 18 March 1890, Kaiser Wilhelm immediately summoned a group of senior advisors around him to announce the name of the new Imperial Chancellor. It goes without saying that consulting or even informing the Reichstag had not entered the Kaiser's mind. When Wilhelm II chose to appoint Leo von Caprivi, a Prussian general, as Bismarck's successor, he told him right from the beginning that his position would be temporary as he did not see a future for the office of chancellor. He merely needed someone to help him manage political affairs until he had gained enough experience and grounding with the German people to rule as an absolute monarch with advice from his inner circle. But as it turned out, Caprivi was his own man and saw the reality of German politics through Wilhelm's naive pipe dreams of a new age of absolutism.

Leo von Caprivi was an interesting choice. After two decades of leadership by the towering figure of the founding father of the German Empire, Bismarck was a hard act to follow. Caprivi was far removed from being a like-for-like replacement. An army general with a distinguished military record, Caprivi had made a name for himself as an efficient and level-headed organiser. He proved to be one of the most talented disciples of Chief of Staff of the Prussian army, Helmuth von Moltke, and thus rose quickly through the ranks. His appointment as Chief of Staff of the Tenth Army Corps in the Franco-Prussian War at the relatively tender age of 39 caused considerable debate. However, Caprivi soon showed he was up to the job and gained the respect of many in the army alongside much public recognition. After the war, he worked in the Prussian War Ministry and in 1883 moved sideways to head the German Navy as *Vizeadmiral*. Interestingly, when Wilhelm ascended to the throne in 1888 and it became evident that he dreamt of expanding the German navy to rival that of Britain, Caprivi disagreed with this so much that he felt compelled to resign, moving back to his old position in the army. Bismarck approved of the principled Prussian officer and his views on restricting German naval ambitions to defensive purposes in Europe rather than expanding it to a force that would roam the world and clash with Britain and France in the process. Thus Bismarck applauded Caprivi's appointment as his successor.

As the American historian Robert Massie describes, Caprivi was 'the model Prussian officer'. He was a 59-year-old bachelor who had led 'a Spartan life': he 'did not smoke, and had few intimate friends and few enemies. He read history and spoke fluent English. His movements were quiet, his manner open and friendly, his language sensible.'*

As such, he seemed to fit the role of transitional chancellor well. A safe pair of hands with a good reputation and a proven track record of efficient management. No doubt Wilhelm also imagined that the Prussian officer in Caprivi would make him an unquestioningly loyal servant of his king, unlike the stubborn and single-minded Bismarck. But it also was no coincidence that the receding hairline, the bushy white moustache and big round shape of his head made him a rather close likeness of his predecessor. Wilhelm thought he had found a subservient administrator in the shell of a bombastic chancellor – the perfect combination that would ease the transition from constitutional monarchy to personal rule. Not for the last time, Wilhelm would prove to be a lousy judge of character.

Caprivi's chancellorship got off to a good start. He told the *Berliner Tageblatt* newspaper that he saw it as his task to 'lead the nation back to normality after an era of great men and great deeds',† acknowledging that he had no desire to be a reincarnation of his predecessor but that he would instead drive a steady course to stabilise Germany internally and externally. This suited all sides: the German public, Bismarck and Wilhelm himself. On Christmas Day 1890, after nine months of Caprivi's chancellorship, the Kaiser wrote to his grandmother Queen Victoria: 'We are getting on well with Caprivi. [...] He is already adored by friends and revered by the opposition. I think he is one of the finest characters Germany ever produced.'‡

★   Massie, p.112.
†   Quoted from Ekkehard, p.949.
‡   Massie, p.113.

As Wilhelm's strong desire to be loved by his people was one of his main priorities, he sought to actively break with Bismarck's aggressive anti-socialist course, and Caprivi agreed that conciliation was the way forward. Together they embarked on a 'New Course' of domestic policy that was intended to end the class struggle and unite the German Empire internally.

The general election of 1890 had shown that the SPD was now the largest party in terms of the popular vote (although this amounted to under 10 per cent of Reichstag seats due to the skewed constituency system that favoured large but sparsely populated rural areas over the dense, urban strongholds of the proletariat who voted for the SPD). The trend was clear, and if Wilhelm wanted parliamentary consent for increased spending on his naval projects, he would have to get German workers on side as well as the ever-popular Catholic Centre Party. While technically still in place, Bismarck's anti-socialist legislation was not enforced by the Caprivi regime and was soon allowed to lapse entirely. Thus socialists were free to campaign without restriction, which gave the working classes a political voice. Caprivi also gave in to the Polish segment of the *Zentrum* by allowing the use of Polish in schools where there were few or no German-speaking children. Both measures immediately set a tone of reconciliation after a long era of anti-socialist and anti-Catholic measures.

Caprivi felt that he could go even further in his second year. In 1891 he introduced a whole raft of proposals for social reform. Sunday work was prohibited – a legacy that lasts in Germany to this day – child labour for those under 13 was banned, and women were limited to working a maximum of eleven hours a week in order to help reduce their exploitation as a cheaper workforce. This moderate and conciliatory tone would also apply to his political style as chancellor. Where Bismarck had sought to control every aspect of political life in Berlin to the point where he had banned direct contact of individual ministers with the monarch, Caprivi opened up the cabinet, civil service, Reichstag and Bundesrat to more cooperation and debate. He did not insist on being present at or even being informed of meetings between Wilhelm and individual politicians. Furthermore, he actively encouraged regular meetings between Prussian ministers and their federal counterparts to coordinate policy. He had no strong political allegiance to any political party or creed. Caprivi was instead a moderate and pragmatic chancellor who took a less ruthless angle on realpolitik, making friends where possible but avoiding the *Reichsfeinde* label for political opposition.

Bringing a pragmatic, honest and conciliatory approach to German politics after two decades of fierce infighting and backroom intrigue may seem admirable, but it was also more than a little naive. Allowing the socialists free speech after years of oppression led to raucous and ugly scenes on the streets and in factories, where waves of strikes were met with fierce opposition from factory owners and industrialists. The latter were in agreement with a rising extremist faction in the Reichstag whose behaviour became increasingly radicalised and outlandish given the lack of control after Bismarck's departure. Often appearing in uniform, radical members of the Conservative Party would close meetings with 'a deafening "Heil!" to the Kaiser'* and generally adopt ritualised behaviour to show their strong support for hierarchical and monarchical structures. These radicals won the day in a rift with moderate conservatives in the party. From 1892, conservative members of the Reichstag were of an altogether more right-wing, anti-Semitic and unpleasant ilk. Financially and politically backed by the powerful Agrarian League, which was formed in 1893, this made for vocal and

---

*   Clark, *Wilhelm*, p.75.

dangerous opposition. Unlike Bismarck, Caprivi simply did not have the political stomach for permanent strife.

Caprivi was also no Bismarck when it came to foreign policy. Herbert von Bismarck, the Iron Chancellor's son and disciple, had resigned as Foreign Minister only days after his father had left office and thus left behind a complicated and confusing tangle of foreign policy agreements. Out of the Kaiser's inner circle of sycophants a replacement emerged in the form of Baron Adolf Marschall von Bieberstein, but the man had little diplomatic experience or tact. Caprivi's own direct and honest style was also no good when it came to creating a compelling mix of threats, intrigue and promises to uphold the fragile peace in Europe against the conflicting interests of Austria, Russia, France and Britain. Caprivi sighed and declared that 'Bismarck was able to juggle with three balls, but I can only juggle with two.' Upon becoming chancellor, he was still blissfully unaware of the secret Reinsurance Treaty with Russia that his predecessor had so cunningly engineered behind the Austrian back, but this was due to lapse in June 1890, and a decision would have to be made. The big risk was that if Austria found out about this secret agreement of its ally and its enemy, the Austro-German relationship would break. On the other hand, letting the agreement lapse would drive Russia into French hands, as the Russian Foreign Minister Nicholas Giers had explicitly threatened. An added difficulty was that, unbeknownst to Caprivi, the Kaiser had already reassured the Tsar that he would see the treaty renewed shortly after Bismarck had resigned. Of course, he did not tell his new chancellor as much. So when the decision was made not to renew the agreement, the Russians felt humiliated. Strained diplomatic relations followed.

Another difficult decision that had to be made was on Germany's economic problems with export and trade all the while that the Tariff Act of 1879 was still in place. In addition to

the artificial barrier to German exports this posed, grain shortages in Germany had also led to rising food prices. This, in turn,
put significant pressure on living costs. A solution to all of these
problems was to lower the tariffs. So Caprivi negotiated a series
of trade deals with Austria, Italy and Belgium in the winter of
1892,* followed by agreements with smaller countries in the
next two years. This, of course, angered the conservative lobby
and their friends in the Agrarian League. Using anti-Semitic
and anti-capitalist rhetoric, they denounced the chancellor's
policy as an attack on German industry and agriculture while
allowing a supposedly globalised Jewish financial elite to erode
German values with their greed. As long as he still had the
Kaiser's backing, Caprivi could just about afford to ignore this
chauvinist clamour, but in 1894 he would irrevocably fall out
with the monarch and the conservatives.

The year 1893 thus marked the beginning of the end for
Caprivi. A military man himself, he intended to modernise
and strengthen the army with a reform package that he introduced to the Reichstag. The standing, peacetime army would
be increased by 84,000 men in exchange for a reduction in
compulsory military service from three to two years. When the
Reichstag refused to pass this, Caprivi dissolved it and elections
returned candidates more willing to go with the proposal. At
first, this seemed a success, but the military elites in Wilhelm's
inner circle despised the meddling in the structures of the army,
and they began a vicious and coordinated campaign against
Caprivi. Wilhelm held on to his chancellor for a while, but when
workers' strike action and SPD success in the 1893 elections
showed an alarming growth in socialist sentiment, Wilhelm and
Caprivi fell out over the best response. Caprivi urged the Kaiser
to make more concessions while the Kaiser had got bored with

---

*   Kitchen, p.182.

the failed attempts to appease the workers and wanted aggressive action to suppress the movement. Wilhelm had proclaimed
in 1888, '*Je veux être un roi des gueux*' – I wish to be king of
the rabble. However, the 'social Kaiser' had soon grown cynical
and disillusioned over the past four years of trying to placate
the increasingly desperate German proletariat. Now faced with
a wall of opposition from conservatives, royal advisors and the
Kaiser himself, Caprivi's position had become untenable and he
resigned in October 1894. The brief experiment of conciliation
had failed. The 'New Course' was over.

Prince Hohenlohe and the Reshuffle of Power 1894–1900

Finding a successor for Leo von Caprivi was not easy. The
capable and honest officer had at least been a respected figure.
However, he had shown that it was increasingly difficult, perhaps even impossible, to balance the interests of the socialists,
Catholics, liberals and conservatives in the Reichstag; never
mind doing so while keeping the aristocracy, military and
Wilhelm himself happy. In addition, Caprivi's appointment
was intended as an interim solution before the Kaiser would
take over the reins himself. Perhaps the time for personal rule
had come? Wilhelm's almost mystical belief in the inspirational
power of kingship that transcended class, creed and denomination convinced him that he would be able to achieve what
Caprivi and Bismarck had not and unite the quarrelling
Germans behind his black, white and red banner. But in order
to do this, national greatness had to be aspired to. A German
Weltmacht – world power – would be an irresistible source of
collective national pride. That was where Bismarck and Caprivi
had gone wrong. 'Old Europe' was too small to hold Germany's

ambitions. Had it not already outgrown its European neigh-bours by almost every given measure? The next chancellor would not stand between Wilhelm and his people or between Germany and *Weltmacht*.

A candidate who seemingly fit the job description was Chlodwig zu Hohenlohe-Schillingsfürst. 'Uncle Chlodwig', as Wilhelm called him,* was closely related to the Kaiser (Wilhelm's mother-in-law was Hohenlohe's cousin). The young Kaiser had known him since childhood and thus used the informal *du* to address him. This and the fact that many of his other relatives held influential positions in government made him a reliable tool for the extension of royal power into the constitutional system. His 75 years – not much younger than Bismarck – also worked in his favour, as Wilhelm did not want a young and ambitious chancellor with a career to build but a 'straw doll' to put up in the Reichstag until he had reformed the system. Hohenlohe also made a great compro-mise candidate for all the warring factions in the Reichstag. A Frankish Catholic, he represented southern interests and might even be able to mend bridges to the Centre Party. On the other hand, he had been in favour of a Prussian-led Germany since 1848. He had also supported Bismarck's *Kulturkampf* as he was opposed to ultramontanism, the idea that the Pope was the highest moral authority on earth, and the Pope's aggressive call for Catholic resistance, which had made him a traitor in the eyes of many in the Centre Party. A political moderate, he had sat in the Reichstag as a liberal as well as a free conservative and was now without party membership, which Wilhelm hoped would allow him to build working majorities as chancellor. In 1885, Bismarck had appointed him as governor of Alsace-Lorraine as it was expected that his Catholic background and moderate

---

*   Stolberg-Wernigerode, p.488.

manner would help reconcile the angry French-speaking populations with their membership of the German Reich. He had not been particularly successful but had proved loyal, and so in many ways seemed to be just the man for the job.

Hohenlohe was not exactly elated when Wilhelm recalled him to Berlin and asked him to become Imperial Chancellor. Knowing full well that the Kaiser was looking for a sock puppet, Hohenlohe pleaded that he was too old for the job, physically and mentally not up to it and not a great public speaker. In addition, he did not have the independent funds to sustain himself in the position. Wilhelm waved all of this aside, promising the chancellor a salary of 120,000 marks per year* out of his own pocket, thereby making the Hohenlohe utterly dependent on his patronage.

Straight after his appointment in October 1894, Hohenlohe's first task was one he had misgivings about: pressing new anti-socialist laws through a Reichstag that now contained forty-four raucous socialists, who had been elected by nearly a quarter of German voters. The text of the legislation was careful to mention only anarchists by name. Otherwise, it talked of 'those who questioned the basis of state and society'.[†] Nevertheless, it was clear to all and sundry that Wilhelm was fed up with being the 'King of the rabble' and wanted to bring the unrest on the street and in the factories to a brutal end. When the Reichstag shot the legislation down in 1895, Wilhelm flew into a rage. He demanded that the Reichstag be dissolved, martial law introduced and a coup d'état planned that would once and for all bring an end to this ridiculous situation that prevented the monarch from executing his divine will. Hohenlohe urged the Kaiser to reconsider, pointing at resistance to such measures

---

*   Baumgart, p.58.

†   Nonn, p.69.

by the southern states and, of course, the German people themselves. Germany would fight a bitter internal civil war while the Franco-Russian agreement, which Caprivi had not been able to prevent in the wake of the lapse of the Reinsurance Treaty, threatened a nightmare of coalitions that might destroy Germany. The Kaiser finally saw reason and his straw-doll chancellor proved to have more of a spine than anticipated, but this would cost him what little room for manoeuvre he had. The political reshuffle that would follow the debacle over the anti-socialist laws would sideline Hohenlohe and lead to the pinnacle of Wilhelm's personal rule.

When on 18 January 1896 Wilhelm spoke to the German people at the celebrations of the twenty-fifth anniversary of the proclamation of the German Empire, he told them that 'The German Reich has become a *Weltreich*' – a world empire. The socialists responded with a mix of ridicule and anger. This proved two things once and for all to the Kaiser: the SPD were a bunch of 'fellows without fatherland', as has often been claimed, and a political system that allowed them leverage was madness. While tied to the constitution, Wilhelm could not just pass legislation without the Reichstag's consent, but he could appoint and dismiss individuals from political offices. Against the strong advice of his chancellor, Wilhelm began to appoint arch-conservatives and sycophants into many political offices both in Prussia and at federal level. These were supposed to implement his will but often proved, in turn, to follow their own agendas and manipulate the Kaiser.

Wilhelm thus appointed into powerful offices many members of his own inner circle, his *camarilla*, also sometimes known as the Liebenberg Circle after Philipp zu Eulenburg's estate in Brandenburg. The key figure here was Bernhard von Bülow, who was appointed as Secretary of State for Foreign Affairs in 1897. Like Eulenburg, Bülow also had a penchant for all things romantic and had charmed the Kaiser for years with his sleek mannerisms and clever manipulation. As Secretary of State, he was technically subordinate to the chancellor. However, from the outset, an agreement between Hohenlohe and Bülow was struck whereby Hohenlohe would keep the poisoned chalice of the chancellorship for as long as he could while Bülow would take charge behind the scenes. Wilhelm had instructed him that it would be his task to build a German fleet, expand German power abroad and do both without provoking war with Britain. 'Bülow will be my Bismarck,' Wilhelm famously exclaimed, hoping that his chancellor too could pull off the impossible foreign policy feat. Bülow was joined in this task by Alfred von Tirpitz, who was appointed as Secretary of State of the German Imperial Naval Office in 1897. With his iconic forked beard, he certainly looked the part and played right into Wilhelm's infantile fascination with naval power. Between 1897 and 1914 he would pursue an extensive policy of building Germany's naval power to where it would be one of the largest in the world, second only to Britain. This *Flottenpolitik*, which was supposed to be diplomatically managed by Bülow, would become the focal point of Anglo-German friction in the build-up to the First World War.

The most influential figure in Wilhelm's inner circle, however, was undoubtedly Philipp zu Eulenburg, whose hold over the young Kaiser did not stem from his political talent, influential relatives or even from direct access. His connection to him was 'emotional rather than spatial',[*] and in fact, he avoided proximity to the court in Berlin and preferred to see Wilhelm in recreational contexts. Twelve years older than Wilhelm, Eulenburg became an emotional pillar to the young Kaiser, a confidant seemingly untainted by the political

---

[*] Clark, *Wilhelm*, p.103.

intrigues in Berlin. Someone who shared his interests in romantic poetry, mysticism and the occult. 'With a shotgun over [his] arm and a songbook in [his] hand',* Eulenburg became a closer political advisor to Wilhelm than anybody else in his inner circle. He deftly created a feeling of emotional intimacy and genuine friendship that played to a yearning in the young Kaiser for the mentor he had never been able to find in his father or Bismarck. While this friendship was genuine, it was also a political tool for Eulenburg. Presenting his close friend Bülow to Wilhelm as the right candidate for Secretary of State, and eventually chancellor, led directly to these appointments. In fact, when Bülow was summoned to Berlin in 1897 to receive his first post, he interrupted his train journey there to see Eulenburg on the way and ask for advice as to how to best deal with Wilhelm.

So was Wilhelm entirely in control by 1900? He certainly liked to think so. Increasingly presenting himself as an emperor of a Germany on its way to *Weltmacht*, he openly talked of personal rule. He saw himself as the personification of the nation. 'World Power became an extension of his Divine Power to rule',† and he had appointed all the relevant ministers and advisors to make it happen. He was truly at the centre of things, or so he believed. Bülow cleverly reinforced the Kaiser's perception, openly admitting that he would happily make himself an instrument of 'personal rule'. Eulenburg too was always keen to stress to Bülow that he must merely guide Wilhelm towards the right path and never seek to force it. Together they cleverly exploited the young king's inconsistencies, lack of political understanding and need for reassurance. Hohenlohe had been sidelined, and

---

*   Eulenburg in a letter to WIlhelm. Quoted from Clark, *Wilhelm*, p.104.
†   Massie, p.141.

Kaiser Wilhelm increasingly saw himself as leader of a world empire.
Portrait by Heyden around 1900.

it was clear to all that Bülow would succeed him and merely play the constitutional game while it was actually Wilhelm's will that would be enforced.

However, as Christopher Clark has comprehensively shown, replacing ministers with his own candidates did not bring about a new age of absolute monarchical power. No amount of ministerial reshuffle could magic away the Reichstag, which still held the purse strings to the military budget and controlled the passing of legislation. Wilhelm could simply not embark on a *Weltpolitik* course or expand the German navy without the consent of the elected representatives of the German people. The latter voted in ever-increasing numbers for the SPD, which became the single largest party in the Reichstag in 1912, and could thus not simply be ignored. Had Wilhelm tried to force a more centralised, personal regime on Germany, the fragile union of states would have fallen apart, and a very real possibility of civil war would have emerged. It was simply impossible to keep Germany united and force it under the Kaiser's heel entirely. Wilhelm had to accept this reality for now.

In addition to the pressure from below, the monarchy was also hemmed in by the elites. The *camarilla* had a powerful emotional and political stranglehold over Wilhelm despite giving him the impression that everything was done with his consent. Besides, the military leadership became increasingly bold and added their voices to the clamour of industrialists, *junkers* and pressure groups. It seemed to Wilhelm that the only common denominator was *Weltpolitik*. If he could lead a path to German greatness and fulfil Germany's potential as a *Weltmacht* in a way that Bismarck and Caprivi had not dared, German workers, elites and political rivals would soon all fall in line. It was the only way.

Weltpolitik: The Search for a Place in the Sun

'[W]e believe it is inadvisable, from the outset, to exclude
Germany from competition with other nations in lands with
a rich and promising future.
('Bravo!')
The days when Germans granted one neighbour the earth,
the other the sea, and reserved for themselves the sky, where
pure doctrine reigns –
(Laughter – 'Bravo!')
those days are over. We see it as our foremost task to foster
and cultivate the interests of our shipping, our trade, and our
industry [...]
In short, we do not want to put anyone in our shadow, but
we also demand our place in the sun.'

Bernhard von Bülow, then foreign secretary, in a Reichstag
debate on 6 December 1897.

Bülow's speech about German colonial ambitions in the
context of the internal power reshuffle has often been interpreted as a watershed moment in German foreign policy.
Where Bismarck and Caprivi had been keen to restrict
German ambitions to continental domination, Wilhelm and
his acolytes dreamt of a German colonial empire and set the
wheels in motion to build one. This is mostly true. As we have
seen, Bismarck was at pains to stress over and over again that
Germany was 'saturated' as a European power and Caprivi
continued this course even to the point where he gave up his
position as chief of the navy when it was demanded of him
that he build this up in order to pursue colonial aims. This contrasted indeed with the open and vocal support for *Weltpolitik*
after 1894 from government circles, the *camarilla* and the Kaiser

himself. But the realities of German expansion painted a different picture. It was under Bismarck's tenure in the 1880s that most of the German colonies, such as they were, had been acquired. Adolf Lüderitz, a businessman from Bremen, bought the first German territory in South West Africa, which he later extended until it spanned the entire coastline from South Africa to Angola, a total of 220,000 square miles. Acquiring some of this territory by swindling a tribal captain out of a much larger area than the latter thought he had agreed to, he quickly became infamous as the 'Lügenfritz' (lying Fritz) and Bismarck came under pressure to act. With the 1884 elections coming up, the chancellor gave in to mounting public pressure and placed Lüderitz's African lands under German 'protection', avoiding the term 'colony' for diplomatic reasons. Thus German South-West Africa marked the beginning of German overseas expansion. In the same year Togo, Cameroon and German East Africa (now Tanzania, Burundi and Rwanda) were added, while Bismarck hosted the Congo Conference in Berlin, which was intended to coordinate European domination in Africa. The following year, in 1885, Pacific territories were added.* It is thus by no means the case that Bismarck forbade all overseas expansion. He simply did not have the means to stop this as German businessmen and other private interest groups pressed ahead and bought land of their own accord. The difference from the post-Caprivi regime was, however, that there was open discouragement of such endeavours and a concerted effort from the government to reassure France and especially Britain that Germany was no rival in Africa and Asia. As is evident from Bülow's speech to the Reichstag in 1897, the tone had changed considerably since then. Germany would no longer shy away from competition with the other powers,

---

*   Kretzschmar, p.10.

and it would not stand by while it slipped into mediocrity on the world stage.

Bülow delivered this speech in the context of controversial expansion into China. The leasing of the territories of Kiautschou/Jiaozhou was under debate to serve as a German naval base in East Asia, and it was evident that this would undermine relations with Great Britain. Arguing that Germany was now a large and powerful nation on its way to overtaking all its European rivals economically, the regime saw no need to avoid such friction at all costs and pressed ahead with the deal. On 6 March 1898, the lease was agreed upon with China. *Weltpolitik* was now in full swing. While nowhere near as critical to the Germany economy as the British and French empires were to their nations, the German colonial empire was a frightening prospect. The thought of German warships parading through the Channel, past British and French coastlines, on their way to territories in Africa and Asia did not appeal to either of the two world powers.

Neither Bülow, nor Hohenlohe, nor Kaiser Wilhelm were able to muster the diplomatic skill of Bismarck and thus they allowed tensions and suspicions to rise. It is rather symbolic that the former chancellor and Reich founder died in the midst of the unravelling of his careful foreign policy network. On 30 July 1898 Bismarck passed away. Delirious from the fever that his untreated gangrene had caused, he muttered that he was hoping to see his dear wife Johanna again (she had died four years earlier). Thus 1898 marked the end of the Bismarckian vision for Germany's future, symbolised by the founder's death and actualised by his successors.

The acquisition of colonies that, however small, now spanned continents necessitated a significant expansion of Germany's naval power. If the colonies were to be held and protected against local insurgencies as well as rivalling European powers,

Germany would need a swift and powerful navy that could strike quickly and effectively. The deterrence value alone would be worth the investment. This line of thought was by no means exclusively German. All European states and many powers further afield such as the USA and Japan began massive naval programmes in the 1890s and Germany would have stood alone had it not followed suit. There was a general, worldwide conviction that to restrict oneself to land forces meant political mediocrity in the medium and long term. This went hand in hand with the increasing nationalist sentiment of the time. Emphasising what was best for one's own country scored political points in the western democracies and internationalism was despised as subversive and unpatriotic. Naval shows, military parades and other shows of national strength were hugely popular and helped keep votes favourable. As Christoph Nonn has pointed out,* where Germany differed from the other powers was its weak starting position, which compared somewhat unfavourably with its enormous economic and geopolitical weight. Just as the French and British empires had begun to stagnate along with the speed of their industrialisation, everything seemed to accelerate for Germany at an alarming rate. The projection of such trends looked bleak for the older powers, while it looked irresistibly promising from a German perspective. Even supposedly lesser naval nations such as Italy and the USA had significantly larger fleets than Germany in the 1890s. This had to change. From 1898 a major programme of naval expansion rolled into gear. Under the leadership of Admiral Alfred von Tirpitz, Germany embarked on a fateful course of *Flottenpolitik*.

The connection between empire and naval strength, or between *Weltpolitik* and *Flottenpolitik*, was long established

---

★   Nonn, p.72.

Kaiser Wilhelm and his sons in naval uniforms.

among scholars, politicians and military strategists around the world. Alfred Thayer Mahan, an American naval officer, summed it up in *The Influence of Sea Power Upon History*, in which he argued that whoever rules the sea also rules the world. Published in 1890, it quickly became not just a favourite of Kaiser Wilhelm's but an obsession. He wrote to a friend, 'I am just now not reading but devouring Captain Mahan's book and am trying to learn it by heart. It is on board all my ships and [is] constantly quoted by my captains and officers.'* Admiral Tirpitz was another avid fan and had Mahan's words translated into German in 1898. Convinced that the book was so good that nobody could fail but be persuaded by it, he circulated 8,000 free copies in an attempt to build public pressure on the Reichstag to pass the First Naval Law in 1898. This law authorised the building and perpetual maintenance of sixteen battleships. Despite the enormous costs and strong opposition from SPD and conservative quarters, the majority of the Reichstag was convinced by Tirpitz's so-called 'risk' strategy. The idea was that Germany would not be able to rival Britain's naval power in the immediate future, and Britain, in turn, would not freely accept German naval expansion. So the solution was to build up sea power sufficient to be too risky to attack. Tirpitz proposed that this risk factor would be reached at two-thirds of the British naval force, which would then pressure Britain to forge an alliance with Germany rather than oppose it.

This worked for a short time as Britain and Germany could find common ground in colonial matters, but ultimately the interests of both nations proved to be irreconcilable. Britain was happy to support German naval ports in East Asia and Africa, but it was not willing to risk French enmity by agreeing to an open alliance with the Reich. Cooperation broke down

---

*   Quoted from Massie, p.xvii.

in 1902, and in 1904 Britain entered an Entente Cordiale with France over policy in North Africa. Egged on by Bülow, who had become the chancellor in 1900, Wilhelm began a clumsy attempt to drive a wedge between the two countries. In the spring of 1905 he travelled to the French colony of Morocco, where he rode through Tangier on a white horse before declaring that the Sultan had his full support to pursue independence from France. It was hoped that Britain would encourage this weakening of French interests in North Africa. Instead, Germany found that only Austria supported its cause while every other nation supported France at the Algeciras Conference a year later, which had specifically been called to settle the issue. The First Moroccan Crisis seemed to lay bare German meddling in Africa and confirmed the Entente Cordiale. Italy and Russia had also built closer ties to France, and Germany found itself increasingly isolated.

In this context, Tirpitz found it easy to argue that the path of diplomacy had failed and that his 'risk strategy' provided the only viable protection for an increasingly isolated Germany. The Second Naval Law, which proposed scaling up shipbuilding by three additional battleships a year until the German fleet had doubled, sailed through the Reichstag. This, in turn, worried the British, who began work on a new type of battleship, the Dreadnought, which was said to be as powerful as two or three regular ships. When Tirpitz caught wind of this, he took action without informing the chancellor or the foreign office. He proposed a third bill to the Reichstag that envisioned an additional spending of 35 per cent when compared with the Second Naval Law and the building of two dreadnoughts and one armoured cruiser a year. After initial resistance from the Reichstag, the feeling of indignation after the humiliating Moroccan Crisis was enough to stir up national sentiment to a point where the passing of the bill became a matter of patriotic duty in 1906. A fourth Naval Law in 1908 eventually sparked a

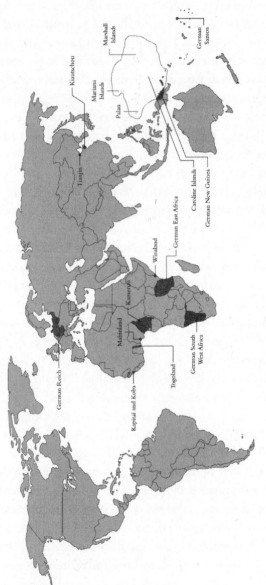

The German Colonial Empire in 1914.

budget crisis that contributed to chancellor Bülow's fall, and a debate ensued in Germany whether the country had not over-stretched itself with the shipbuilding programme.

Despite a monumental financial effort, Germany was losing the naval race with Britain and had instead only sparked anger and suspicion among the European powers. In 1912, the new German chancellor, Theodor von Bethmann-Hollweg, eventually ended the naval build-up and tried to forge an alliance with Britain, but it was too late for that. Britain had nothing to gain from such a situation but a lot to lose. Germany's navy was large but not large enough to pose a serious threat. In 1914 Britain had twenty-nine dreadnoughts while Germany had seventeen, its overseas empire was still the largest in the world by far, and France and Russia were more important allies than Germany. Germany also still had closer economic ties to British colonies than it had to its own, which had largely proved financially fruitless. Thus *Flottenpolitik* and *Weltpolitik* gained Germany a small array of colonies and the second-largest navy in the world in exchange for diplomatic isolation and looming economic catastrophe.

Kultur

As meagre as the achievements of German colonial policy may have been in terms of land gain, they nonetheless had a huge psychological impact on the German people. *Kolonialwarenladen*, literally a 'shop for colonial wares', became a synonym for 'corner shop' that lasted well into the 1970s,* by which pre-viously exotic goods such as coffee, chocolate, tobacco, sugar, spices and tea had long become everyday items. From 1890,

---

*   Thielke, in Klussmann, Ch. 4.

these colonial goods were widely available in German shops and advertised with increasingly evocative labels, showing elephants, palm trees, exotic fruit or racially stereotyped depictions of African tribesmen. The desirability and consumption of such products rose enormously. By 1914, Germans accounted for one-third of worldwide coffee consumption,[*] second only after the USA, which had 30 million more inhabitants. Germans were proud of their colonial empire and it caught the imagination of children and adults alike.

This colonial enthusiasm went hand in hand with a broader trend of nationalism that had evolved from its liberal roots in the middle of the century to a more aggressive 'friend–foe'[†] concept by 1900 and beyond. The liberals had seen nation states as political constructs that would act as guarantors for the rule of law. But they now became political as well as cultural, ethnic and racial rallying points. The concepts of survival, struggle and competition in the natural world, which Charles Darwin had popularised in his 1859 book *On the Origin of Species*, also published as *The Preservation of Favoured Races in the Struggle for Life*, began to be seen as a universal law that applied to humans as much as plants and animals. In this Social Darwinist world, where only the strongest and fittest survived, nation states and their peoples were pitted against each other in a perpetual struggle for resources, space and ultimately survival. This intermingling of the concepts of nation, people and race found its conceptual outlet in the word *völkisch*, which self-appointed linguistic hygienists such as Hermann von Pfister-Schwaighusen even suggested as a replacement for the word 'national' as the latter had its origins in Latin, not German. The *völkisch* movement then began to identify each nation on ethnic and racial grounds,

[*]   Rischbieter, Ch. 6.
[†]   Wehler, p.105.

not linguistic and cultural ones as the liberals had. The Anglo-German philosopher Houston Stewart Chamberlain formalised the ideological foundation for this in his hugely influential 1899 book, *The Foundations of the Nineteenth Century*. He stressed the continuation of Ancient Greek and Roman sophistication in the modern Western and particularly Germanic populations of Europe:

> Certain anthropologists would fain teach us that all races are equally gifted; we point to history and answer: that is a lie! The races of mankind are markedly different in the nature and also in the extent of their gifts, and the Germanic races belong to the most highly gifted group, the group usually termed Aryan [...] Physically and mentally the Aryans are pre-eminent among all peoples; for that reason they are by right [...] the lords of the world.*

If nations are thus defined on ethno-racial grounds, minorities become at best parasites, at worst enemies. Chamberlain describes Jews as 'newcomers' to the European world from the 'Near East'. Page after page of his book shows the supposed differences in skull structure, facial features and general physique, which were depicted as outward signs of an inherently different race of inferior character and disposition. Following this line of argument, anti-Semitic organisations such as the Pan-German League and elements of the arch-conservative right developed a virulence in their rhetoric against Jews that bordered on calls for genocide. Everyday anti-Semitism became acceptable in large swathes of the population and made a mockery of civil equality.

---

*   Chamberlain, p.542.

In this climate of angst around the survival of the Germanic race, to not support the Kaiser, colonial expansion and later the war effort became a potentially fatal act of treason. Socialists, Jews, national minorities and other supposedly internationalist elements were seen by many as a danger to the internal and external security of the Reich. This could be utilised in elections and policymaking. Wilhelm and his chancellors thus found it possible to push naval and military expansion programmes through a Reichstag increasingly dominated by socialists even though this came at the expense of social reform. Kaiser Wilhelm himself had a famous penchant for all things military and thus lobbied for educational reform in that direction – a rare example of political initiative. Speaking to a conference for teachers and education officials, Wilhelm explained that the curriculum needed to produce 'vigorous men who will also be intellectual leaders and servants of the Fatherland'.* This went hand in hand with the traditions of the *Turnbewegung*, a gymnastics movement dominated by Friedrich Ludwig Jahn, an early German nationalist and educator. Both saw a strong connection between physicality and nationhood, which found an ideal outlet in militarism and the defence of the fatherland.

Thus many Germans, including the Kaiser himself, developed a curiously romantic vision of the military that was interwoven with the concepts of Social Darwinism and defensive nationalism. Due to the special role that the military had played in unifying Germany from liberating German lands from Napoleonic rule to the unification wars, soldiers held a special status in the popular imagination. Romanticised images of brotherly camaraderie founded in the blood relations of the ethnic-German community were reinforced in the years

---

*   Quoted from Clark, *Wilhelm*, p.83.

of compulsory military service that every German male had to undergo.

The now infamous incident of the so-called Captain of Köpenick epitomises this perfectly. An unemployed cobbler by the name of Wilhelm Friedrich Voigt with a long criminal record decided in 1906 that the blind German belief in military structures could be exploited. He bought used items of a captain's uniform from different shops and wore them on the morning of 16 October to see how far they would get him. He marched to his local army barracks and told four grenadiers whom he found there to come with him. He picked up six more from the local shooting range, and together the group went on a train journey to Berlin Köpenick, where Voigt told 'his' soldiers to occupy the town hall. The authority of his uniform was not only enough to commandeer the soldiers around, but he also told the local police to keep law and order while he went about his important business. Voigt had the mayor and the treasurer arrested (for supposed fraud) and confiscated 4,000 marks (with receipt!) before he told his soldiers to split into two groups, one taking the prisoners to the Neue Wache in Berlin for questioning, the other to stand guard at the town hall. He then changed back into civilian clothes and disappeared. This ridiculous episode may be a one-off, but it serves to exemplify the obedience and respect a German army uniform commanded at the turn of the century.

Hand in hand with the love for the military came a general longing for order, discipline and stability. Most ordinary Germans approved of the strong police interference in everyday life (police officers even picked up truanting children and returned them to school). The tone for this was set by the many ex-army men from whom the force largely recruited. Despite this, the elites still became uneasy at the thought of losing control over the population as a whole as people began to have spare time on their hands. While in 1871 German workers still laboured in their factories and fields for an average of seventy-two hours a week, by 1914 this had steadily fallen to fifty-five hours.[*] At the same time real wages had risen by a quarter between 1885 and 1913. With more time and money at their disposal, Germans suddenly had the means to enjoy themselves and the first signs of a mass culture began to develop with or without the elite's consent. While as early as 1890 Wilhelm was worried that a reduction of working hours bore 'the risk of encouraging idleness',[†] mass culture and communication via new media could not be stopped. As Rein Traub has shown, the Franco-Prussian War had catapulted the medium of the postcard into mass use out of nowhere. What started as field correspondence home became commercially so lucrative that art reproductions quickly became popular motifs and were not only sent to loved ones but also kept as images, hung on walls and given as presents. As urbanisation and the development of photography developed, both city and landscape scenes became a new trend. Many scholars have claimed that this led to an overall phenomenon of the 'aestheticisation' of daily life. People wanted to have beautiful things around them and cared about their furniture, fashion and neighbourhood.

Educational reforms had produced an enviable literacy rate of 99 per cent, one of the highest in the world, which meant that even the poorest wage worker could find some liter-ary relief after a long shift. The proportion of the population that can be described as avid readers rose from an estimated 5 per cent to 30 per cent between 1850 and 1900.[‡] Much to the dismay of the Kaiser and the elites, the often repetitive and

---

[*]   Schroder, p.287.

[†]   Quoted and translated from: Traub in Klussmann, Ch. 5.

[‡]   Ibid.

hard labour in urban factories did not usually inspire the reading of Goethe's poems or other such lofty fare. Most yearned to escape into different worlds – exciting daydreams to flee the monotonous routines of their working day. Pulp fiction novels became popular, either as cheaply produced copies to buy or in factory libraries, which many industrialists began to install. Some were also printed as serials in newspapers. The most loved genres, as ever, were romance, crime, adventure and sentimental drama, but Germans also developed a curious fascination with Wild West stories. Karl May's *Winnetou* trilogy, which was published in 1893, became an instant bestseller. Until 1899, he had never travelled to any of the exotic settings of his adventure stories from the Wild West to the Orient. Still, they fascinated him as much as they did his audience and his books sold 200 million copies worldwide, half of which were sold in Germany alone. May's work more than anything exemplifies the desire of his contemporaries to relax, to be entertained and to enjoy.

Meanwhile the elites, including the otherwise so forward-looking Wilhelm, saw art and culture as a means to build and preserve national identity. He began to patronise nationalist artists such as the Anton von Werner, who had produced the paintings of the proclamation of the German Reich. National monuments too were commissioned en masse. Wilhelm I had been modest and withdrawn, but after his death in 1888, he was no longer in the position to object to his mythification. Nearly 400 monuments were built in his honour,[*] the most impressive of which was the National Kaiser Wilhelm Monument in Berlin, created by his grandson's favourite sculptor, Reinhold Begas. Over 700 Bismarck memorials were built, a process that began as early as the 1860s but saw rapid acceleration after the old chancellor's death in 1898. The so-called Bismarck Towers

---

[*]   Ullrich, *Nervoese Grossmacht*, p.360.

were the most popular design, and of the 234 that were built, 173 are still standing. Perhaps the most iconic symbol of how both elites and ordinary people were unified in their love of escapism, adventure and war culture was the *Völkerschlachtdenkmal* in Leipzig. Over 500 steps lead up the 300ft concrete tower, which has supposedly been built on the site of the bloodiest encounter with Napoleon's troops. Completed with both public and private funds in 1913, the colossal structure looms over the surrounding plains and remains a popular tourist attraction to this day.

Wilhelm and the conservative elites were less close to their subjects when it came to musical and literary tastes. Richard Wagner's operas were deemed to be inspiring, patriotic and educational with their tales of Germanic heroism and Wilhelm had developed a personal taste for them even before he became Kaiser. A member of the Potsdam Wagner Society, he was in personal contact with Cosima Wagner, the composer's second wife, who had organised the Wagner Festival in Bayreuth after her husband's death in 1883. While Wagner's work was influential in the upper echelons of society, workers, who by 1907 made up three-quarters of German employees, were less taken by the genre.

While there were obvious and increasing cultural and ideological rifts between the social classes in Germany by 1914, there were still also a whole range of unifying elements. Most Germans shared a love for order, discipline and the military. The latter combined strongly with a romanticised vision of camaraderie, loyalty and adventure, which found its outlets in the pulp fiction of Karl May and the high culture of Wagner. Concepts of struggle, fraternity and foes created a powerful bond between elites and workers, who were otherwise so bitterly opposed. It was therefore no surprise that Wilhelm and his chancellors instinctively turned to such concepts as the only means to create consensus between 1898 and 1914.

Bülow and Bethmann-Hollweg: The Search for Consensus 1900–14

'Bülow will be my Bismarck,' the Kaiser had exclaimed in 1895, pinning all his hopes of domestic and foreign political success on the charming diplomat. But Bülow was no Bismarck. True, he had a certain self-confidence and elegance about him that had opened the doors to a successful diplomatic career. Still, contemporary observers felt that there was little substance behind the suave facade. Referred to as the 'Eel' by some of his colleagues, 'this slender young man with his round, friendly face, his smiling blue eyes and his carefully trimmed moustache'* had managed to charm his way into Wilhelm's inner circle. This was in part due to the fact that he shared a love for all things romantic, mystical and esoteric with the Kaiser and his best friend, Philipp zu Eulenburg. The latter had not only recommended him for the office of foreign secretary but also for the chancellery when both felt that the time was right for old Hohenlohe to go. In 1900 Hohenlohe was 81 years old and increasingly frail. He had been a mere 'shadow chancellor' for some time with Bülow calling the shots as foreign secretary. Frustrated to be a sock puppet for politics he disagreed with and fatigued by the toll this took on his body and mind, the old chancellor resigned, and Bernard von Bülow became the new Imperial Chancellor on 17 October 1900.

From the outset he inherited the same irreconcilable political divisions his three predecessors had struggled with.

---

*   Massie, p.185.

The ever-increasing presence of the SPD in the Reichstag would make budget approval for the ballooning costs of the naval and military expansion projects a difficult undertaking. The only solution was to unite the other political parties in a bloc large enough to pass the desired legislation. Bülow called this concept *Sammlungspolitik*, a policy of 'bringing together'. He explained that 'the basis of imperial domestic policy must be one that is as broad as possible, so that there is room for conservatives, national liberals, moderate clericals [i.e. Centre Party supporters] and reasonable left-liberals.'* This, he figured, would help with both national unity and the fight against 'the social revolution'.† The latter was a spectre that frightened not just Bülow but many other members of the elite. The SPD had begun to make links to the more left-leaning wing of liberals, finally enabling them to translate their advantage in the popular vote into more seats in the Reichstag. August Bebel opened the party up to realpolitikal aims such as a shortening of the working day and more democracy. These were achievable through reform rather than revolution and required cooperation with other parties and the imperial regime. However, there was still much socialist rhetoric in use, which called for a revolution of the proletariat. This odd mixture of practical realism and radical ambition stemmed from the party's Erfurt Programme of 1891, which in itself reflected the two wings of the party and called for both revolution and reform. In either case, the SPD had become a powerful and dangerous source of opposition to the establishment and the other political parties would have to be bribed and beaten into unified action to combat this.

---

*   Quotes translated from Winzen.
†   Ibid.

This worked reasonably well with regards to *Flottenpolitik* aims. The naval officer corps, in contrast to the army, had evolved into a mostly bourgeois institution in terms of the background and culture of its personnel. The conservatives thus frequently spoke of the 'ghastly fleet', which they despised not only for its culture but also for its role as an instrument of free trade and capitalism. Nonetheless, the conservatives could also agree that naval expansion was necessary for German colonial ambitions. A majority for naval funding could therefore always be cobbled together so long as enough concessions were made. The disagreements did not so much lie in *whether* the German fleet should be extended but *how*. One source of revenue was tariffs on imports. Bülow went ahead and in 1900 he effectively banned the import of meat, using another outbreak of the plague in Russia as an excuse. He knew this would please the conservative, land-based elites and their representatives in the Reichstag. Their support for the 1902 Tariff Act was guaranteed. This increased the customs on imported grain even further and thus in theory also state revenue. The problem was – and here Bülow's political clumsiness was apparent – that Centre Party votes for this had to be bought with the promise that the revenue would be used for social projects such as the Fund for the Support for Widows and Orphans. Catholic votes increasingly haemorrhaged out to the SPD, and the Centre Party leadership were hoping to retain at least some with such charitable measures. Thus tariffs had been introduced but did little to alleviate the looming financial crisis caused by the mushrooming military and naval expenditure. Tactically, the move was also a complete failure. In the 'Tariff Elections' of 1903, the rising food prices caused by Bülow's policy became the top issue and all the parties that had supported the regime were punished; the SPD came away with a spectacular 31.7 per cent of the vote.

With further tariffs politically unpalatable, financing the mounting costs of *Weltpolitik* became a real headache for Bülow. The only remaining option was taxation. But indirect taxation in the form of a VAT-like charge on goods and services would have hit workers and the poorest disproportionately. This was therefore out of the question for the SPD and the *Zentrum*. Many liberal voters too were appalled at the rising prices the tariffs had caused and would not have allowed their parties to make things even worse. The only option was to tax the rich. In 1906 Bülow found a majority for a fiscal reform programme that included a progressive inheritance tax. Bizarrely the situation had pushed Bülow into a *Sammlungspolitik* that did not bring together the conservative parties against the SPD and its allies, but the other way around. For the first time, the Reichstag had proved it could act in the interests of the majority of people and against the elites. Aristocratic landowners suddenly had to give up some of their wealth to a state that funded pensions, benefits and mass education. In this context, the regime had to further agree to salaries for Reichstag members and thus economic independence for MPs. When the government brutally crushed an uprising of the Herero and Nama tribes in its African colonies, the SPD and Centre Party blocked funding for colonial purposes unless the Reichstag was given a say in its use. Bülow had truly let the genie of democracy out of the bottle.*

At the end of 1906 there was a brief downward trend in food prices and the public grumbling began to quieten down. Bülow used the situation cleverly and dissolved the Reichstag for re-election. Socialist voices were crying in the wilderness of an emphatically pro-colonial atmosphere. The chancellor styled the entire election campaign effectively as a referendum on German colonial pursuits and was rewarded with loud approval

---

*   Nonn, p.80.

from the electorate. The pro-government parties did well while the SPD lost almost half of its seats. Suddenly, finding consensus in the Reichstag was significantly easier, and the first formal coalition was built, the so-called Bülow Bloc. This was an uneasy alliance of the conservative and liberal parties that only really had one thing in common: *Weltpolitik*. Both sides were happy to see Germany expand its influence in the world, the former for ideological reasons, the latter for economic ones, but every other bit of legislation was passed in tit-for-tat haggling. The liberals got a law that allowed women to become members of political organisations but in exchange the conservatives got a bill that made the disowning of Polish landowners easier. Thus Germany ambled along politically with no sense of direction other than its *Weltmacht* ambitions. The Bülow Bloc eventually collapsed in 1909 when further financial reforms were required to pay for this and conservatives and liberals could not agree on how the necessary taxes should be sourced. Now that he had lost control of the Reichstag completely, Bülow's position had become untenable. He handed in his resignation, and on 7 July 1909 his deputy took over.

Theobald von Bethmann-Hollweg was a modest, loyal and calm individual. He stood in good stead with his Kaiser through his own dealings with Wilhelm but also on the strength of rec-ommendations from the members of the *camarilla*. Friedrich August von Holstein had pulled many strings behind the scenes ever since Bismarck's dismissal and recommended the new chancellor. Bethmann-Hollweg's brief was to calm the agita-tion in the Reichstag and come up with a workable plan to fund the now exponentially rising costs of naval, military and colonial expansion. Fittingly described by Michael Stürmer as a 'Hamlet character',[*] Bethmann-Hollweg was indeed in a tragic

---

[*]   Stürmer, *Key Figures*.

position whereby his own considerable intelligence and political acumen stood in contrast to the unstoppable tide of events that built around him. Tearful and desperate at the fate that awaited him, he pleaded with the leader of the Reich chancellery to persuade the Kaiser not to appoint him. 'Only a genius or a man consumed by ambition could ever want such an office,' he lamented to a colleague. 'And I am neither.'* But as a Prussian civil servant his first instincts were loyalty, duty and dignity, and he accepted the office without complaint once the decision had been made.

In an attempt to rebuild the Bülow Bloc, which he had helped engineer in his time as deputy chancellor, Bethmann-Hollweg followed a policy of careful reform. The antiquated three-tier voting system in Prussia had been a particular bone of contention. The uneven weighting of votes preserved conservative control in Prussia, despite the state's heavily urbanised population and growing SPD-voting proletariat, and with that came conservative domination of the Bundesrat, the upper chamber. Any reform of Prussian local voting therefore meant reforming the direction of federal policy as well. But the issue could no longer be ignored, with loud pro-SPD demonstrations and strikes on the rise. Thus Wilhelm's increasing military and colonial ambitions required some social and political reform if funding was to be acquired without the strikes and demonstrations on the streets ending in civil war. In 1910 Bethmann-Hollweg suggested a re-weighting of the votes rather than abolishing the tiered system altogether. Soldiers and academics would get more of a say. This was aimed to show the Social Democrats that progress was being made and appease the conservatives and liberals by lending more political

---

★   Quoted and translated from Egelhaaf, p.123.

weight to their protégés. In the end it was a compromise that pleased no one and a frustrated Bethmann-Hollweg withdrew the motion after much acrimonious debate. Meanwhile, rising food prices caused by the tariffs, frustration with the lack of political reform and increasing indirect taxation to fund the military programmes led to vocal anger in the ever-growing urban population of the German workers. They eventually made their voices heard in the 1912 election, which can only be described as a landslide victory for the SPD. Gaining over a quarter of all seats, it became the single largest party in the Reichstag and had to be worked with if legislation was to be passed. This in turn frightened and angered the conservatives, who became ever more defensive and stubborn in their refusal to grant reform.

Thus the last two years before the outbreak of the First World War became a period of stagnation. What Christoph Nonn has described as a 'stable crisis'* was indeed a two-year period without too much outward upheaval, but it was also one of a frustrating stand-off in the Reichstag. The latter certainly made an impression on contemporaries, who perceived the time from 1912–14 as a time of crisis. When the First World War eventually broke out in the summer of 1914 it was not in small part accompanied by hopes that once again political acrimony could be overcome through pan-German unity. Perhaps the deep fissures in the German political soul could once again be moulded together in the fires of war? Bismarck's famous words rang true once more in many German ears: 'Not through speeches and majority decisions will the great questions of the day be decided [...] but by iron and blood.'

---

*   Nonn, pp.88–92.

A Scandalous Kaiser

To contemporaries and later observers alike, Wilhelm has been an outrageous and fascinating man. Described as a 'fabulous monster'[*] by a British biographer even during his lifetime, the Kaiser was seen as a tragic figure by sympathisers, as a prisoner of his times who was misunderstood and manipulated by those around him. Less sympathetic commentators have seen in him a megalomaniac, from the historian Ludwig Quidde's infamous and thinly veiled depiction of Wilhelm as a modern Caligula[†] in 1894 to the civil servant Hermann Lutz's assessment of the Kaiser's 'periodical insanity'.[‡] Whatever people's feelings towards the monarch, it was hard to be indifferent. Where his father and grandfather had both been agreeable orators but had largely reserved their public appearances to selected, formalised occasions with pre-written speeches, Kaiser Wilhelm II became a media monarch, courting the press in an almost modern sense. Restlessly, he travelled from town to town, showing himself to as many people as possible. Between 1897 and 1902 alone, he made 233 visits to 123 different towns[§] where he gave speeches that would often be printed in the newspapers afterwards and thus discussed nationwide rather than just locally. Acutely conscious of this, Wilhelm would spend hours at a time scanning the papers for comments about him. He could also become very upset when even small details were inaccurate or had been embellished by journalists.

---

[*]   *Fabulous Monster* by J. Daniel Chamier, 1934.

[†]   Caligula – Eine Studie über römischen Cäsarenwahnsinn.

[‡]   'Wilhelm II. periodisch geisteskrank! Ein Charakterbild des wahren Kaisers' by Hermann Lutz 1919.

[§]   Clark, *Wilhelm*, p.221.

The unfortunate combination of Wilhelm's desire for publicity and his sensitivity to it was completed in its potential for disaster by the fact that he was 'singularly ill-suited to the communicative tasks of his office', as Christopher Clark put it.* Wilhelm I and Frederick III had understood that it was the role of a modern monarch to represent the country while experts wrote speeches, made policy and forged diplomatic networks. By contrast, Wilhelm II naively imagined that he could restore the royal authority and pomp of bygone centuries, 'always taking a piece of the Middle Ages with him',† in the words of a contemporary court official. Thus his frequent interferences in domestic and foreign policy were dreaded by those who sought to manage and mitigate their impact. Wilhelm's desire to act independently and communicate directly with his subjects thus collided with his unfortunate ineptitude to strike the right tone, find suitable words and analogies and present himself in accordance with expectations. One cannot help but observe similarities to certain modern politicians who, frustrated with the desire of their staff to soften and tone down, take to social media to communicate directly with the public. The panicked attempts by spin doctors and spokespeople to mitigate the effects of this by way of issuing public statements of explanation and 'clarification' is amusingly reminiscent of Imperial German diplomats sending hurried telegrams to offended foreign dignitaries or Bülow's frantic issuing of rewritten scripts of Wilhelm's speeches to the press before they published his actual words.

Thus Wilhelm's tenure was set up for scandal right from the beginning. His impromptu speeches not only lacked professionally written scripts but were often not even planned. The

---

*   Ibid., p.227.

†   Quoted and translated from Herre.

most infamous example of such spontaneous communication is the so-called 'Hun Speech' of 1900, where Wilhelm addressed troops in Bremerhaven who were just about to sail to China to suppress the Boxer rebellion. Racially charged rumours of atrocities of local fighters against German colonists had gone through the press and the Kaiser, in a typical misjudgement of the public mood, thought he spoke for all Germans when he struck a fiery, chauvinistic tone:

> Should you encounter the enemy, he will be defeated! No quarter will be given! Prisoners will not be taken! Whoever falls into your hands is forfeited. Just as a thousand years ago the Huns under their King Attila made a name for them-selves, one that even today makes them seem mighty in history and legend, may the name German be affirmed by you in such a way in China that no Chinese will ever again dare to look cross-eyed at a German.*

Conjuring up the image of tribal hordes pillaging, raping and murdering their way through peaceful civilian settlements was not the sort of thing that was expected of the commander-in-chief of a modern European military force. At best it could be seen as ill-judged historical analogy, at worst a call for unlawful and inhumane methods of warfare. Recognising the potential for ridicule and outrage, Bülow (then foreign secretary) quickly issued a revised version to the press editing out the entire 'hun' section but, as with all of Wilhelm's public blunders, the trouble was that thousands had heard the speech in person and their own version quickly made the rounds. August Bebel, the leader of the SPD, publicly sneered in the Reichstag that the allusions to the huns had 'for some reason' disappeared from the official

---

*   Kaiser Wilhelm's Hun Speech.

printed script of the speech. Writing in the 1920s, Bülow would later call this speech Wilhelm's worst, but of course by then his view would have been shaped by the British use of the word 'hun' during the First World War.

Such verbal clumsiness combined unfavourably with the Kaiser's own self-consciousness to make him a figure of satirical ridicule in a way that neither Bismarck nor Wilhelm I had to endure. The hours spent in the careful 'training' of his famous moustache just served further to make him the perfect motif for political cartoons, which usually depicted him as naïve or infantile. By 1907, Wilhelm had acquired a reputation as a whimsical, outrageous and somewhat foolish young monarch who stood in sharp contrast to his dignified old grandfather. Nonetheless, republicanism was confined to a radical political niche. Most Germans continued to support monarchical rule and found a place in their hearts for their eccentric Kaiser.

The scandals that hit Wilhelm in 1907 and 1908, however, were on a completely different scale and seriously damaged his position and authority. The nightmare began for the Kaiser when a journalist called Maximilian Harden published a series of articles between April and November 1907, in which he accused Wilhelm and his inner circle of pacifist tendencies that weakened Germany's international standing. In order to lend his accusations weight, Harden played into contemporary perceptions of homosexuality, which equated same-sex attraction with moral weakness. His articles made a number of thinly veiled accusations against various members of Wilhelm's inner circle from Eulenburg to Bülow, insinuating that their meetings at the Liebenberg estate were of a homoerotic and amoral nature. Having found out that the French diplomat Raymond Lecomte dined there at a private meeting shortly after the humiliating First Moroccan Crisis, Harden saw his fears confirmed. Clearly Wilhelm's friends had conspired with the

French to humiliate and weaken the Kaiser and his imperial ambitions. An effeminate and weak clique of personal advisors tainted Wilhelm's foreign policy and he needed to be separated from them. Thus Harden became more and more explicit in his articles and political cartoons until the matter could no longer be kept quiet and Wilhelm found out about the accusations. Sensitive to public commentary as he was, Wilhelm could not let the matter be and demanded that it be settled in court (homosexuality was a crime under Article 175). All those tainted by the scandal were to be dismissed. This was a huge mistake. What would have likely been a short-lived rumour started by a political magazine now became a public spectacle of five separate court cases that dragged on over the next two years, and in Eulenberg's case until his death in 1921. In order to preserve his own reputation, Wilhelm tried to cut all ties with those accused. He asked Bülow to resign as chancellor as soon as it was feasible and even broke his long and close friendship with 'Phili' Eulenburg. Despite the Kaiser's deep emotional links to the circle, Wilhelm, who was rumoured to have had numerous affairs and even extramarital children, was unlikely to have suddenly developed a homosexual relationship and thus few people believed him to be directly involved. As Eulenburg's wife bitterly observed: 'My husband gets beaten but the Kaiser is the aim.' Thus Wilhelm's reputation remained relatively intact but the political consequences of the affair cannot be understated. Having lost his entire political and personal support, the insecure Kaiser looked for new advisors and found them in the military circles that surrounded him at court. Thus Harden had inadvertently pushed Wilhelm into the arms of the Prussian military hawks who had preached for years that a European war was inevitable and deemed Bismarck's and Caprivi's caution futile. The imperial head would now be filled with stories of German greatness, sea power and the struggle for national survival. Looking back after the First World War, Harden himself later called the Eulenburg Affair the biggest political mistake of his life.

The year 1908 would see an even more serious political crisis, which this time involved the monarch directly. On 28 October, the British *Daily Telegraph* published an interview with Wilhelm that caused outrage in Germany. Nearly a year earlier, he had spent a three-week holiday at Highcliffe Castle in Dorset, where he chatted with his host Edward Montagu-Stuart-Wortley about Anglo-German relations. The latter wrote up a summary of these conversations in interview style and sent it to the newspaper which, as per protocol, sent a copy of the transcript to Berlin for approval. Wilhelm, now bruised by the Eulenburg scandal and prior public embarrassments, left the matter entirely to Bülow and his staff, trusting their political and diplomatic expertise. According to Bülow expert Peter Winzen, the chancellor was on holiday at the time and thus did not read the transcript. Instead he passed it on to press officer Otto Hammann, who was unfortunately also on holiday. Thus the document landed on the desk of a junior clerk who did not feel authorised to alter the Kaiser's words. He approved the text as it was. So it was that the Kaiser's raw and unfiltered words, spoken in the context of a private conversation on holiday, entered the public domain with explosive effect. The most infamous line, 'You English are mad, mad, mad as March hares', was accompanied by claims that Wilhelm belonged to an anglophile minority in Germany, which was a dangerous claim in the context of *Flottenpolitik*. In addition, Wilhelm bragged that his strategic ideas won the British the Boer Wars, that his foreign policy in Asia was aimed against Japan and not Britain, and that he alone had prevented Franco-Russian action against British interests in South Africa. The interview was thus offensive to most European nations and their rulers, Japan, the German political class and, of course, the German public itself, who the Kaiser had presented as largely anglophobic.

In the immediate aftermath of the crisis, Bülow's position as chancellor became untenable. Not only was he tainted by the Eulenburg scandal but he had lost the Kaiser's trust. He resigned and was replaced by his deputy, Theobald Bethmann-Hollweg. The Kaiser himself was shell shocked. Having done everything correctly this time, he felt betrayed, bitter and alone. For two weeks he fell into a deep depression and the strain of the situation took a huge toll on his mental state. The final straw came at a hunting party in Donaueschingen where a strange and bizarre spectacle would push the fragile Kaiser over the edge. Wilhelm's friend, General of the Infantry Dietrich von Hülsen-Haeseler, thought he would lighten the mood by dressing up as a ballerina. Much to the amusement of the Kaiser and the assembled guests, the portly old man daintily danced and whirled across the floor in his little pink tutu. Just as the hysteria and laughter had torn even the glum Kaiser out of his brooding, the general was suddenly seized by a heart attack. Clutching his chest and with his face contorted in pain, Hülsen-Haeseler collapsed and died on the spot. A terrible silence hung in the room. What would the press make of this? What would this look like when the dust of the Eulenburg scandal had not even settled? The general's body was quickly stripped of the pink evidence that testified to the circumstances of his embarrassing death and the matter was hushed up. But Wilhelm could not take another blow. He suffered a nervous breakdown. When he finally recovered his strength, he found that he had lost a lot of public trust and feared that any additional incidents would damage the German monarchy irrevocably. He thus kept his head down and was not seen or heard in public for months. His first official speech did not occur until the summer of 1910, and even from then on, his public appearances took on a muted and formal tone. Public scandal was largely avoided between 1909 and 1914, but the Kaiser's confidence had been hugely dented and he allowed himself to be gagged and dominated by his new circle of advisors.

Thus the last years before the First World War were marked by a lack of political leadership and direction. A reluctant chancellor with no wish to hold the office and no vision for Germany's political future received no instructions from his brow-beaten Kaiser. The latter in turn had lost his political circle of advisors, his old mentor Bismarck and had few friends left. Thus a wide power vacuum existed at the top of a nation that was economically powerful, armed to the teeth and in internal and external conflict. Ulrich Wehler called the First World War Germany's 'escape forwards'[*] and in 1914 it seemed indeed to be the only way out for a nation stuck in a political cul-de-sac. The stage was set for military power to step out from behind the curtain and take centre stage.

---

[*]   Wehler, Ch. 8.

5

CATASTROPHE 1914-18

'One day the great European War will come out of some damned foolish thing in the Balkans.'

Otto von Bismarck in 1888

The Spirit of 1914

Sunday, 28 June 1914 was a beautiful summer day in Sarajevo. Heir presumptive to the Austro-Hungarian crown, Franz Ferdinand, and his wife Sophie, Duchess of Hohenberg, had been invited to inspect troop manoeuvres in the provincial capital of Bosnia and Herzegovina. It was a special occasion in many ways. The 28 June marks *Vidovdan*, a crucial religious and national holiday to the Serbs. Wanting to promote a positive and peaceful image of Austrian overlordship over the province, as well as signalling potential for reform once he became emperor, Franz Ferdinand was keen to show himself in the best possible light. The day also marked the couple's fourteenth anniversary and offered a rare chance to celebrate their marriage in public. Sophie did not hold the required rank to be considered a proper match for the heir to the Austro-Hungarian throne, so court protocol banned her from most public occasions.

Franz Ferdinand had married her anyway, for love. He had to renounce any claims to the throne for his children with Sophie, and therefore effectively cancelled his own royal blood line so he could be with her. On this occasion they would get a rare opportunity to enjoy each other's company, free from the snobbery of the world at court. For at Sarajevo, he had been invited in a military capacity and not as heir presumptive. So Sophie could be by his side as his wife without the suspicion that she was acting as queen consort in the making.

While parading in an open-topped car on their way to Sarajevo's City Hall, the couple was attacked by a 19-year-old extremist by the name of Nedeljko Čabrinović, who hurled a grenade at them. The driver accelerated when he saw the object coming at them, and the bomb exploded under the next car, injuring sixteen people but leaving the royal couple unharmed. Franz Ferdinand and Sophie were quickly hurried to the City Hall, where they arrived shaken but determined to see the victims of the attack. After brief and awkward ceremonial proceedings, they left for the hospital.

And that would have been the end of this dramatic day, had not their driver taken a wrong turn. Franz Ferdinand's adjutant, who stood on the footboard to shield the party from further attack, noticed the driver's error and told him to stop and reverse. The driver hit the brakes. In one of the most tragic coincidences in modern European history, the royal party came to a halt right in front of Gavrilo Princip, another member of the Black Hand gang, who had planned the assassination attempt. Fate had delivered their targets back to him, just when he had given up. Princip had stood at a street corner outside a delicatessen shop, dispirited with the way the royal couple had escaped his friend's grenade with their lives. Now he looked up at them and could not believe his luck. The driver was frantically trying to find the reverse gear, and the car's grinding protests were accompanied by the Archduke's complaints about the delay. Princip had a golden opportunity. He drew his pistol and walked up to the car, a manic glint in his eye. He pulled the trigger. Once, then twice before he was overwhelmed by Franz Ferdinand's men. Sophie turned to look at her husband, who was bleeding profusely from a gaping hole in his neck. He looked back into the beautiful pale face he loved so much and cried, 'Sophie! Don't die! Live for our children!' Neither had realised the other bullet had also met its target and hit Sophie in the stomach. Both were dead within the hour.

With this tragic story began an unravelling of events that would lead to the outbreak of the largest war the world had ever seen. The precarious interplay between the highly militarised and industrialised nations of Europe had become a tinderbox by the summer of 1914. The assassination provided the spark. The First World War would cause 40 million casualties, wreck the European economies and create human suffering on an unimaginable scale. It would also bring the German Empire to its knees.

Wilhelm received news of the assassination on board the *Hohenzollern*. The Kaiser loved to use the royal yacht in the summer for shorter trips as well as extended holidays to Norway. On 28 June 1914, he was hosting a tea party on deck for senior officers and their families. In the midst of the festivities the fateful telegram arrived, bringing news of the murder of Wilhelm's friend, the Archduke Franz Ferdinand. Wilhelm immediately returned to Berlin to deal with the aftermath. It is clear from the Kaiser's private comments and his marginal scribblings on the relevant documents that he believed an Austrian reckoning was in order and should be supported. His remark that, '[t]he Serbs must be swept up, and right soon"* has often been interpreted as a wish to provoke a major war, but it is much more likely that the Kaiser simply deemed a localised conflict between Austria and Serbia the most probable outcome, not a general European war. While it is true that he asked the Prussian Minister of War, Erich von Falkenhayn, whether the army was ready for war regardless of the outcome of the diplomatic efforts, he was also keen to keep Russia and the other European powers out of the situation. This was the strategic thinking behind his assent for the famous 'blank cheque', which promised Austria military support. Throwing the weight of the second largest (after Russia) and most advanced land army of the world behind Austrian aggression in Serbia was meant to localise the war by deterring Russia from entering. It was not an attempt to start a world war. In fact, Wilhelm was still so relaxed about the situation that on 6 July he went on his planned summer cruise to Norway, taking his beloved dachshunds Hexe and Dachs with him – hardly the actions of a bloodthirsty warlord waiting for the outbreak of the largest conflict mankind had ever seen.

There is no doubt that Wilhelm's military advisors saw the possibility of a much larger war. They were at best accepting the risk, at worst actively working towards it. Chief of General Staff Helmuth von Moltke had argued for some years that the European power balance was shifting eastwards. The balding military man fancied himself one of the best strategic minds of his age, but the shadow of his famous uncle and namesake loomed large. Helmuth von Moltke 'the Elder' had been Chief of General Staff of the Prussian Army for thirty years, in which time he led the successful campaign against France in 1870 and modernised the forces strategically and technologically. Styling himself Moltke 'the Younger' in order to draw parallels with

---

*   Quoted from Clark, *Wilhelm*, p.281.

Kaiser Wilhelm on a holiday cruise on board the *Hohenzollern*,
25 July 1914.

his famous uncle, the nephew viewed the situation in 1914
as his opportunity to shine. He told Wilhelm that the dreaded
Russian 'steam roller' would eventually see the emergence of

overwhelming military power, at which point it would be too late for Germany to react. Moltke's advice in July 1914 was thus 'Now or never!'* The military elite had spent years convincing themselves that a general European war was inevitable. The question was not if, but when it would happen.

Bismarck's old nightmare of coalitions was on their minds, and so planning for the eventuality of a two-front war went a long way back. When Alfred von Schlieffen was appointed as Chief of the General Staff in 1891, he spent years working out a strategy in the event of a war with France or Russia – or both. Germany's position in central Europe suited it well economically, but it also made it vulnerable to attack. By the time he was replaced by Helmuth von Moltke in 1906, Schlieffen's ideas had undergone various revisions, but the principle remained the same: in the eventuality of a looming two-front war, Germany would attack France with overbearing force. The bulk of the army would then be transferred to the Eastern Front, where they could face the slower but larger Russian forces. In contrast to Schlieffen, Molkte was somewhat more concerned about the strength of the French and Russian armies. He argued that both had developed in size as well as speed of mobilisation. If they were given the slightest notice of impending war, the plan would fail as time was of the essence and a strong French response would bog down the German army enough for Russia to attack from the other side. The terrible but logical conclusion in the eyes of the military elites was that a pre-emptive strike on France might be the only way to win a European war.

On 28 July the Kaiser returned from his holiday cruise to find that Austria-Hungary had declared war on Serbia. In line with the usual diplomatic war dance, all the European powers reacted. Britain let chancellor Bethmann-Hollweg know that

---

*   Thamer, p.11.

their neutrality was unlikely and that they would probably be obliged to support France and Russia if it came to it. When full Russian mobilisation was ordered on 30 July, everything that Molkte had preached for years seemed to unfold. In the logic of the Schlieffen Plan, every minute was crucial. Give Russia and France any more time, and Germany would find itself in a two-front war it was unlikely to win. A pre-emptive strike on France was the only way. And so it was that Germany declared war on Russia on 1 August and on France two days later, even though the latter had seemingly nothing to do with the trouble in the Balkans. Britain's war declaration on Germany followed on 4 August. The First World War had begun.

'Mood jubilant. The government has managed brilliantly to portray us as the ones who are being attacked.'* These were the words Chief of the Imperial Naval Cabinet, Karl Alexander von Müller, wrote in his diary and they showed the cynical attitude of the military elites towards the supposedly 'defensive war' that Germany had allegedly been forced to enter. They also hit the nail on the head as far as public opinion went. Chancellor Bethmann-Hollweg had been largely successful in convincing the Reichstag and the German people of the idea that Germany was the injured party. There were mass demonstrations for peace in Berlin and other German cities but they blamed mainly Austria and partially Russia for their warmongering over the assassination. As historian Jeffrey Verhey has shown, the myth of unabated jubilation all across the German lands must be dispelled. Germans were anxious and by no means keen to sacrifice life and limb for European power politics. Nonetheless, the defensive spin on the situation created an atmosphere of defiant patriotism, the so-called *Augusterlebnis* (August experience). As Hans-Ulrich Thamer put it, there was a 'conflicting

---

★   Quoted and translated from Thamer, p.21.

mix of apocalyptic threats and hopes, of individual expectations and longings'* but the ideas that this war was forced on
Germany and that it provided a chance for the fatherland to
prove itself appealed to many.

Germania by Friedrich August von Kaulbach, August 1914.

---

*   Ibid., p.25.

The illusion of a defensive war was crucial and had to be upheld for as long as possible. Bismarck understood this when he provoked the Franco-Prussian War in 1870 just as much as the political establishment did in August 1914. In this way, it would be possible to overcome the internal strife, division and stagnation that had plagued the country for years, once more binding all Germans together with blood and iron. On the day that war was declared on Russia, 1 August 1914, the Kaiser stepped on to his balcony at the Royal Palace and addressed his people directly:

> I thank all of you for the love and loyalty that you have shown me these past days. These were serious days like none before them. Should there be battle, all political parties will cease to exist! I, too, have been attacked by one party or another. That was in times of peace. It is now forgiven with all my heart. I no longer think in terms of parties or confessions; today we are all German brothers and only German brothers. If our neighbours want it no other way, if our neighbours do not grant us peace, then I hope to God that our good German sword will emerge victorious from this hard battle.*

In the context of the Social Darwinist worldview that many contemporaries shared, the supposed attack on Germany meant nothing short of a fight for survival for the young nation. What were petty class conflicts, differences in the way one worshipped or where one stood on the political spectrum when compared to the naked survival of the fatherland? By 1914, the Reich had existed for over four decades. The vast majority of Germans had grown up in their nation state as a concept they took for

---

* The Kaiser speaks.

granted. Perhaps the jubilance of the so-called 'Spirit of 1914' was exaggerated by earlier generations of historians, but there is no doubt that the camaraderie, sense of belonging and defiant nationalism triggered by the outbreak of war in August was widespread. Wilhelm's regime enjoyed almost unanimous support for their war, even if only briefly.

The First World War: A Summary 1914–18

The moment Germany had declared war on Russia on 1 August 1914, forces were sent westwards. Attacking France was seen as the best defence. As the Schlieffen Plan was based on the idea that a two-front war could be avoided by fighting on one front at the time, the timing of the campaign was crucial. Schlieffen himself reckoned even in 1905 that Germany would only have three weeks to defeat France before moving troops back to the Eastern Front, where Russian mobilisation would hit twenty-eight days after the beginning of the campaign. In 1914 Molkte had to face the fact that Russian mobilisation had already begun on 30 July. Furthermore, everyone agreed that the French defences along the German border would slow down the invasion too much and thus a corridor through Belgium was chosen for the invasion of France. Troop exercises in 1901 had indicated that this would be successful so long as forty-eight and a half army corps were used, Belgium remained passive and Britain did not get involved. As it turned out, Schlieffen's successor Molkte attacked on 2 August with only thirty-four corps, quickly ran into brave Belgian resistance and Britain declared war on 4 August 1914. Frustrated with the painful loss of thousands of German recruits to coordinated rifle fire and the new Vickers machine guns used by the British Expeditionary Force, as well as fierce Belgian resistance, army discipline began to break down immediately. Early encounters like the Battle of Mons on 23 August, where German casualties were double those of the defending British forces, did not stop the advance but they frustrated its speed. The German army had swelled its ranks from 808,280 to 3,502,700 in just twelve days and thus contained many conscripts and volunteers who were not prepared for the savagery of modern warfare. Breakdowns of discipline led to ugly scenes. On 25 August, troops entered the university town of Leuven, where they massacred nearly 250 civilians and burnt down the library. The image of the German 'hun' pillaging and burning his way through innocent civilian settlements, which Wilhelm had so clumsily conjured in 1900, now took on the form it would retain in British propaganda for the rest of the war.

Despite the brave resistance from British and Belgian forces, in early September, German troops crossed the River Marne and threatened to capture Paris. Encountering fierce French opposition in the First Battle of the Marne from 6 to 12 September (for which General Gallieni had famously requisitioned Parisian taxis to carry 6,000 soldiers to the front line), the Imperial army eventually fell behind the river and dug in. This trench line would see very little movement for the duration of the war and so marked the beginning of the deadly stalemate that became the hallmark of the Western Front. France would not be forced to surrender in weeks, nor indeed at any other time in the First World War. The Schlieffen Plan had failed.

Things did not go as planned on the Eastern Front either. Shortly after the declaration of war on Russia, screams of 'The Cossacks are coming!' could be heard all over East Prussia. Panic was indeed in order. Underestimating the Russians severely, the German High Command had not expected an attack for weeks and yet on 15 August, only fourteen days after the war declaration, the Russian advance began. The Eastern Front was only defended by the 8th Army with the other seven fighting in Belgium and France. The situation looked bleak. Splitting its forces, due to the obstacles of the Masurian lakes, the Russians attacked with 191,000 soldiers from the north and 200,000 from the south, while only 153,000 Germans stood against them. The situation would lead to the meteoric rise of two Prussian generals: Paul von Hindenburg and Erich von Ludendorff, who were barely known outside of military circles until this moment. The Battle of Tannenberg, which raged from 26 to 29 August, was a seemingly miraculous victory for the German army. The second Russian army was obliterated. Its commanding general, Samsonov, committed suicide and 45,000 Russians were captured. Hindenburg and Ludendorff became living legends. In the German psyche, this battle would remain a saving grace within the bleak and humiliating experience of the First World War. It would also create a loophole for the military elites to withdraw from responsibility and to create the toxic stab-in-the-back myths of the 1920s. At the end of 1914 a disillusioned public realised that the war would not be over by Christmas but the glorious victory at Tannenberg gave hope that Germany would prevail, even if it did require more sacrifices than anticipated.

Meanwhile, things looked bleak on the Western Front. After the campaign had ground to a halt at the Marne, both sides repeatedly tried to outflank each other at the northern end of the front line, digging in and moving northwards in the process. This frantic 'Race to the Sea' brought bitter losses. German casualties numbered over 130,000 at the First Battle of Ypres in October/November 1914 alone, while little to no progress was made in terms of land gain. Frustrated and increasingly desperate, the High Command resorted to terrible measures.

On 24 April 1915, 160 tonnes of chlorine gas were dropped on the French army. This causes burning pain, angry red blisters and respiratory problems in its victims, not to mention the psychological effects of panic and horror. Zeppelin bombing raids on Britain began in January 1915 with the explicit consent of Kaiser Wilhelm, who only stipulated that London must be spared lest his relatives in the British royal family be harmed – this was later also abandoned. Unrestricted submarine warfare led to the sinking of the *Lusitania* on 7 May 1915, a British passenger ship with nearly 2,000 civilians on board. These heinous measures had limited military effects but were designed to undermine enemy morale. As Admiral Tirpitz put it, 'The measure of the success will lie not only in the injury which will be caused to the enemy, but also in the significant effect it will have in diminishing the enemy's determination to prosecute the war.'* In reality, all it did was to cement the image of the barbarian 'hun' who sought to destroy all that was decent and civilised in Europe.

The year of 1916 took this industrial war to new and terrible heights. The months of mass slaughter at the fortress city of Verdun, from February to December 1916, would irrevocably burn themselves into the German psyche. Erich von Falkenhayn, who had taken over from Moltke in 1914, had thrown everything at the French defenders at Verdun: 26 million explosive shells, 100,000 poison gas shells and seventy-five divisions of men. It proved once and for all that this was not a heroic effort, man against man, but a war of attrition where human lives were cheap commodities. Referred to as the 'blood mill' by soldiers, the battle became synonymous with the futility of the conflict. Over 350,000 casualties for the German attackers and nearly 400,000 for the French defenders

---

*   Robinson, p.54.

had led to absolutely nothing. The front line remained where it was, the fighting continued. Leaving behind a wasteland of burnt vegetation, craters, mud and rubble, the surviving forces were simply drawn away to the next meat grinder at the Somme.

In order to relieve the French forces at Verdun, a British army that consisted largely of volunteers attacked the German positions at the River Somme in northern France. British Field Marshal Sir Douglas Haig believed that if he used enough force, he might be able to finally break through the German lines and force movement into the stalemate situation. Sending an inexperienced force of young volunteers up a muddy slope through no-man's-land cratered by the preparatory artillery fire ended in disaster. The battle-hardened German troops mowed down the British attackers in wave after wave of machine gun fire. Many of the advancing soldiers got stuck in the barbed wire. Adapted tactics and the first use of tanks gradually levelled the field, but the battle was aborted in November without a clear outcome. With over 3 million soldiers fighting and 1 million dead or wounded, the Somme became the largest battle of the Western Front and one of the bloodiest in human history. Yet it seemed to have achieved no tangible outcome.

This was trumped in scale by the Brusilov Offensive in the east. The Entente powers wanted to provide a coordinated attack, east and west, to bring the Central Powers to their knees. So the Brusilov Offensive provided the counterpart to Verdun and the Somme. While relatively evenly matched in numbers, the attack on 4 June 1916 brought devastating losses on the Austro-Hungarians, who counted 200,000 casualties in just three days. In the end, the battle would cost around 1 million lives on both sides, but the Russians did achieve their aim and broke through, securing one of the biggest victories in the First World War. The Austro-Hungarian appetite for war was gone and they urged Germany to support a peace offer to the Entente Powers. Half-heartedly, the German government agreed but deliberately left the text vague and non-committal. Unsurprisingly, the Allies turned the offer down in December 1916 as it was obvious that Germany would not be willing to make concessions. With millions dead and wounded, too much had been lost on all sides to simply give in now.

The clash of the British Home Fleet and the German Navy at the Battle of Jutland in 1916 failed to end the naval blockade, which was causing severe malnutrition and other supply issues in the winter of 1916–17. Desperate to force a breakthrough, the German High Command decided to resume their unrestricted submarine warfare from February 1917, attacking even unarmed merchant ships without warning. This was the final straw for the US government, which had been urged to scale up support by the British for some time. With their ships now under attack again and resentment over the more than 100 Americans who had died when the *Lusitania* was sunk in 1915 still raw, the war declaration came on 6 April 1917. This marked a turning point in the entire conflict. The stalemate between the European nations was suddenly shaken up by the entry of an industrial superpower. In a war of attrition, victory comes down to the amount of resources and manpower each side can deploy and their willingness to do so. Fresh into the war in its third year, Americans had not lived through the traumas of Verdun, the Somme or the horrors on the Eastern Front. In the summer of 1918, around 2 million US troops would still fight an increasingly fatigued and demoralised German force. With the October Revolution of 1917 signalling the withdrawal of Russia from the war and internal opposition against the Imperial regime mounting, the militaries felt cornered and became defiant. They would get something out of the war, no matter the cost. A last heroic effort would be mounted at the beginning of 1918.

On 8 January 1918, Woodrow Wilson promoted his fourteen-point peace programme to the US Congress in the hope that it might provide a route to peace. But on the same day Leon Trotsky started negotiations with the Germans over a peace treaty that would allow Russia to withdraw from the conflict. Buoyed by the Treaty of Brest-Litovsk, signed on 3 March 1918, the Imperial Government turned down Wilson's ideas. They now had a lot to lose if they were to give up all the eastern territory gained in the war. Brest-Litovsk agreed on the set-up of German satellite states from the Ukraine all the way to the Baltic Sea, with Russia losing more than half of its industrial capacity and nearly a third of its population to Germany.* In the eyes of the High Command, Germany had sacrificed too much to give this all up now.

And they seemed to be proved right. The Spring Offensive, which began only three weeks later, on 21 March 1918, seemed initially successful. Also named *Kaiserschlacht* (Kaiser's Battle) in order to boost morale for what was sold to the soldiers as the last big push, the German lines were pushed 60km west and 90,000 enemy soldiers were captured. However, supply problems were now severe and the offensive had to be aborted. The Allied counteroffensive pushed the German line back quickly in July to almost exactly where it had been in September 1914. Millions of people had lost their lives, four years had passed and nothing had been achieved. On 29 September Hindenburg and Ludendorff finally saw sense and asked the government to negotiate an armistice. On 11 November 1918 this was finally signed and with it the death warrant for the German Empire.

---

*   LeMO.

The Silent Dictatorship

'A united Germany has never been conquered,' Wilhelm had declared in a speech on 6 August 1914, appealing to his people to stand together in the face of an attacking enemy. He stressed that the fatherland was being ambushed by 'a world of enemies' and that nothing less was at stake than the 'existence of our Reich'.* While there was significant enthusiasm for Germany's colonial policy, expansionism was an altogether different proposition when it came at the costs of one's livelihood or even life itself. Farmers were worried that their horses might be requisitioned; women were concerned about their sons and husbands being dragged off to war; people in the cities feared that they might be cut off from food supplies. To ask such sacrifices of the nation, the illusion of a defensive, even beleaguered scenario had to be maintained. The Kaiser and his government were astonishingly successful in this. A contemporary observer noted that, '[o]ne hears again and again: "If the Kaiser had been able to avoid the war, he would have done so."'† Wilhelm enjoyed immense popularity and warm adulation in the early phase of the war in 1914. Even before censorship set in, the press almost unanimously described how the relationship between him and his people had tightened in the face of war.

This temporary feeling of camaraderie applied to the Reichstag as well. Wilhelm famously told the assembled MPs on 4 August: 'I no longer recognise parties, I know only Germans.' He then proceeded to ask them to pledge that they were, 'without respect to party, rank, or confession, determined to go with me through thick and thin, through

---

* Wilhelm's speech, 6 August 1914.
† Clark, *Wilhelm*, p.334.

suffering and death'.* Astonishingly, all the political parties did
so, including the SPD. In a passionate and emotional speech,
leader of the parliamentary faction Hugo Haase declared that
his party would 'not let down our own fatherland in the hour
of need'.† Arguing that he regretted that the imperialist ambitions of the European powers had led to this war, now that
it had become a reality, Germany must be defended. He also
stressed that the despotism of the Russian Tsar in particular
was worth fighting and that this stood not in contrast to the
international working-class movement. The SPD, and the rest
of the Reichstag deputies, therefore unanimously approved
the war credits the government had asked for. Chancellor
Bethmann-Hollweg must have sighed with relief. At a membership of 3 million, trade unions could have done immense
damage to the German war effort at the slightest nod from the
SPD. Mass strikes and demonstrations had already plagued the
country for the last two years, since another economic crisis
had hit in 1913. There were calls for a general strike from radical sections of the movement. But now it seemed there was
no appetite for sabotage from German workers, either on the
ground or from their political representatives.

This phenomenon of temporary domestic peace has been
called *Burgfrieden* – fortress truce. The idea of a besieged castle
fitted perfectly with the defensive image the government was
so desperate to uphold. No matter how many differences separated the inhabitants of the German castle, ultimately they were
forgotten in a fight for national survival. Thus the Reichstag
voluntarily surrendered all of its powers in an Enabling Act.
Elections and campaigning were suspended, parliamentary
meetings postponed indefinitely. The trade unions promised

---

*   Wilhelm's speech, 4 August 1914.
†   Hugo Haase's speech, 4 August 1914.

to abandon all strike action until the end of the war and the day-to-day running of the financial affairs of the country was surrendered to household commissions. Bethmann-Hollweg no longer had to fight arduous battles in parliament but was now able to hold informal talks with the political parties directly and their individual members in the commissions. Democracy had been suspended.

This temporary feeling of goodwill allowed the military to stretch its tentacles into all areas of national and local government. Using Article 68 of the constitution, the army seized executive powers. In peacetime, the country was geographically divided into twenty-five military districts that were normally used to recruit and train army personnel in each area.* Now the commanding officers of these districts became the political leaders there, only responsible to the Kaiser directly. The military had thus completely sidelined the Reichstag, chancellor, ministries and other constitutional structures, and it had done so within the legal framework. It now had control over policing, security, censorship, food distribution, education, transport and every other aspect of government.

The muzzling of the press meant that the German public were getting a very skewed picture of what was happening at the front lines. As the consent of the German public was dependent not only on the defensive nature of the war but also on the notion that it was temporary, the military regime fed people a constant diet of press releases that suggested military success. The grinding stalemate on the Western Front paled in light of the fact that Paris was in reach. Stories of the heroic individuals overshadowed statistics of casualties and death. Wilhelm himself fell victim to this. Isolated behind the thick walls of the *Großes Hauptquartier* in Berlin, he rhapsodised about how 'a

---

*   Thamer, p.38.

sergeant killed twenty-seven Frenchmen with forty-five bullets' and boasted of 'piles of corpses six feet high'.[*] Thus, the 'Silent Dictatorship' of the military remained relatively unchallenged until 1916. Even the parliamentary SPD remained supportive. Only a fifth of their members demanded an end to the war in 1916.[†]

As Christopher Clark has shown, the Kaiser himself became increasingly sidelined. Technically the Commander-in-Chief of the armed forces, he should have provided a focal point for the coordination of sea and land power by setting broad strategic aims. However, the Kaiser knew he was a poor strategist (despite Alfred von Schlieffen letting him win every strategic exercise he had ever taken part in). He voluntarily left the military decision-making first to Moltke and then to Falkenhayn, both of whom, concerned about the constant nervous state the Kaiser was in throughout the war, were somewhat selective in the information they shared with him.

After the spectacular victory at Tannenberg on the Eastern Front, Paul von Hindenburg emerged as a German war hero. He increasingly began to overshadow the Kaiser in the role of somebody who could quell the 'longing felt in some quarters for a Führer whose authority over friend and foe alike would be absolute and undiluted'.[‡] At 6ft 5in, he cut a towering figure and his distinctive face – almost rectangular in shape – made him a recognisable motif for the many drawings, sculptures and memorials that were commissioned all over Germany in his honour. When Hindenburg became overall strategic commander of the German war effort in 1916 and headed the Third OHL (German High Command), it was therefore

---

[*]   Quoted from Clark, *Wilhelm*, p.311.

[†]   Nonn, p.97.

[‡]   Clark, *Wilhelm*, p.336.

easy to use him as a figurehead to legitimise further infringement of democratic and civil rights. Together with his deputy Ludendorff, the duumvirate acquired so much political power that they had to pay little heed to the Kaiser, the chancellor, the Reichstag or anybody else. The Silent Dictatorship was fully set up.

The Hindenburg Programme rolled out in September 1916 effectively created a command economy, solely aimed at fuelling the insatiable demands of 'total war'. With the British naval blockade intact, the supply of food and other essential goods had already been critical before 1916, but now even what remained was requisitioned for the war effort and civilians were left to starve. Besides, 1916 alone had brought a staggering number of casualties – almost 1 million. Censorship could hardly cover the realities of limb amputations, letters of condolence to the wives and children of the fallen or the increasingly desperate postcards from the front lines. Public mood was about to tip and the *Burgfriede* of 1914 would be shattered.

German workers were the first to break the truce agreed between the trade unions and the government. Increasingly desperate during the bitter winter of 1916–17, they began to organise mass strikes even in ammunition factories. With little food available legally, higher wages would at least have allowed them a better position on the black market. But Hindenburg's kudos as war hero still held. When he demanded the resumption of unrestricted submarine warfare in order to break the British naval blockade, this was seen as an act of acknowledgement of the plight of the German workers. The political parties supported the move despite the high risk of a war declaration from the USA. When the latter came in April 1917, all was lost and many knew it. In response, the militaries further sharpened rationing in an attempt to match the immense supplies the Americans would bring to the war. This in turn triggered unprecedented discontent. Mass strikes took place and calls for a conciliatory peace without annexations became louder. Matthias Erzberger, a vocal Centre Party politician and journalist, gave a passionate speech to the Reichstag on 6 July 1917, where he outlined, in forensic detail, just how desperate the situation had become. The only way out was to make peace with the Allies, granting concessions where necessary. Two weeks later, he presented this to the Reichstag formally as a Peace Resolution, which was passed by 212 to 126 on 19 July. Instead of responding to the will of the democratically elected representatives of the people, Hindenburg, Ludendorff and Crown Prince Wilhelm (the Kaiser's oldest son) conspired to blame Chancellor Bethmann-Hollweg, who had been sceptical about unrestricted submarine warfare from the outset. He was forced out of office. It is quite remarkable that at this point neither the militaries nor any of the political parties suggested a replacement. In the case of the former, this was due to a fundamental lack of recognition for democratic structures. The political parties, on the other hand, shied away from the responsibility that came with the chancellorship in such difficult circumstances. Thus it was left to Wilhelm to choose the candidate and he opted for a reliable bureaucrat, Georg Michaelis. He faced a successful vote of no confidence as early as October 1917 and was replaced by *Zentrum* politician Georg von Hertling. The Peace Resolution remained ignored. Its instigator, Matthias Erzberger, drew such hatred from the far right that he would be branded a traitor and brutally murdered in 1921 while out on a walk. Brazenly, elements of the sympathetic, nationalist press jeered: 'He may be as round as a bullet, but he is not bullet-proof.' Politics in Germany had taken an ugly turn.

While most of the Reichstag was now asking for the war to end, they were hopelessly divided on everything else. The Centre Party simply wanted peace, liberals were asking for the three-tier system in Prussia to be abolished, while the SPD were asking for social reform on top of both of the other demands. The latter had also become bitterly divided among themselves. The question that had caused acrimony in their ranks for years, namely whether to work with the government to achieve reform or against it in a revolution, had been brought to a climax by the war. Working with the government now meant supporting a war effort that left millions dead and wounded and many more starving at home. Working against the government meant instigating trouble at home while the fatherland was fighting a struggle for national survival. The party leadership could no longer hold both factions together. The radical left wing broke away. Members who had been expelled from the SPD for breaking party discipline and voting down war credits in 1915 and 1916 formed the Independent SPD (USPD) in April 1917. This new party contained everything from principled pacifists to the radical communists of the *Spartakusbund*. When Russia underwent its revolutions in 1917, they held hopes to replicate the situation in Germany, using the anger and desperation caused by the war. Threatened by the spectre of communist agitation, the military leadership in turn patronised the foundation of the German Fatherland Party in September 1917, a far-right organisation that demanded a *Siegfrieden* – victory peace. They pledged to carry on fighting until land gain and annexations were secured. The war had thus, for the first time in German history, brought about the existence of sizable extremist parties.

As the military situation became increasingly hopeless in 1918 and the Russian example had spooked the elites into believing that a revolution would come if Germany went into another war winter in 1918–19, support for the Kaiser and the military dictatorship waned visibly. More and more Centre Party politicians, liberals and even some conservatives joined the SPD in calling for reform and an ending of the war. In October 1918, Wilhelm gave in to this by appointing the liberal Prince Max von Baden as chancellor. As the heir presumptive to the Grand Duchy of Baden, he was nonetheless deemed a pillar of the aristocratic establishment and therefore a suitable compromise candidate. Prince Max initiated parliamentary reform, putting the Reichstag at the centre of the constitution and using this as the basis for his peace negotiations with US President Wilson. He suggested to Wilhelm that the only way out of the war without a revolution was his abdication. Wilhelm was frightened by the fate of his Russian cousin. Tsar Nicholas II and his entire family, including his young children, had been unceremoniously shot in a basement on 17 July 1918. However, Wilhelm still dithered and toyed with the (unconstitutional) idea of renouncing the German crown but not the Prussian one.

Germany's political landscape remained irrevocably changed and scarred by the First World War. The ease with which the German people had allowed their semi-democratic system to descend into a military dictatorship stood testimony to the fact that parliamentary culture was still in its infancy. In times of crisis, the German people had looked for strong leadership and a Führer figure rather than to their political system. In that they differed from France, Britain and the USA, where rationing, martial law and other restrictions were temporarily in place but did not alter the political foundations permanently. The war had also caused the sharpening of political fault lines. For the first time extremist parties had entered the scene as serious political alternatives to moderate government. The First World War had not only brought down the German Empire but also created social and political disunity. Social imperialism and *Weltpolitik* had failed not only externally but also internally.

The War Economy

'Once peace has been concluded, we can present our enemies with the bill for this war,'[*] declared Secretary for the Treasury Karl Helfferich in a presentation to the Reichstag. As had been the case with Bismarck's war against France in 1870, the plan from the outset was to finance the fighting with loans and bonds rather than higher taxation. After the mass strikes of German workers in the pre-war years, the political establishment was anxious to keep the fragile Fortress Truce established in August 1914. So arguments in the Reichstag over who was paying what seemed unpalatable. Besides, Centre Party and SPD votes for the war credits were dependent on sparing the working class any additional hardship. SPD leader Hugo Haase made this quite clear in his speech on 4 August 1914. Explaining that his party would vote for the proposed war loans, he warned that the government must remember 'the women and children robbed of their providers. For them, fear for their loved ones is combined with the threat of hunger.'[†] Burdening the working classes any further was out of the question. By contrast, the British government was so confident of public support for their involvement in the war that they felt they could tax people heavily. Income tax in Britain rose from 6 per cent in 1914 to 30 per cent in 1918, while the number of people paying it nearly tripled.[‡] Thus the package of loans that the German government proposed on 4 August was entirely geared towards a short, successful campaign that would be financed retrospectively from reparations.

---

[*]   Quoted from Wehler, p.202.

[†]   'Social Democratic Party Statement on the Outbreak of the War' by Hugo Haase.

[‡]   'Taxation during the First World War'. Official figures from www.parliament.uk.

Initially the militaries and their political acolytes claimed that they were well prepared financially. After all, there was the famous *Reichskriegsschatz*, a war chest containing the indemnity payments from the Franco-Prussian War. This was a war chest in the literal sense. It consisted of 1,200 wooden boxes containing shiny gold coins that had never been in circulation. Between 1871 and 1874, the French had paid their reparations in gold, which was melted down, and Goldmark coins were minted. The portrait side featured Wilhelm I in profile and around him were engraved the words 'Wilhelm, German Kaiser and King of Prussia'. The flip side showed the coat of arms of the German Empire. The chests were stored at Spandau Citadel, a sixteenth-century Renaissance fortress on the western outskirts of Berlin. The Julius Tower, which housed the gold, was (and is) one of Spandau's most iconic buildings. A round structure, 30m tall and with crenellations at the top, it conjured up images of medieval castles. Its walls were 3m thick and thus provided a secure place to keep such large gold reserves. The coins had never been used but were brought directly to the Citadel. The thought of gleaming, patriotic gold coins stashed away in the darkness behind the thick walls of a fortress caught the imagination of the public. To this day, the term *Juliusturm* is used to refer to surplus state funds (which has not happened since the 1950s). The *Reichskriegsschatz* was thus ideal propaganda material to reassure the Reichstag and the informed German public that there was a financial cushion. In reality, the coins only amounted to 120 million marks in 1914. The economic historian Hans-Ulrich Wehler estimated that the direct costs for the war amounted to 100 million per day.[*] The glorious war chest would therefore not even have paid for two days of fighting.

---

[*]   Wehler, p.201.

The direct war costs amounted to just under 160 billion marks in total by 1919, only 16 per cent of which was covered by tax revenue. The rest was loans and war bonds. In order to achieve such a vast increase of cash circulation, the government introduced bank notes that could not be exchanged into coins at banks after September 1914. This new paper currency bore no direct relation to the national gold reserves and could be more easily printed and its value adapted as required. In fact, the government would resort to thirteen separate currency reissues during the war, creating a surplus of paper money that rapidly led to the deterioration of the value of the mark. In 1913, you could have bought a US dollar for 4.2 marks; in February 1920, you needed 32.9 marks.[*] Wehler goes as far as to claim that, 'Germany's post-war inflation began in August 1914.'[†] It is easy to see why from 1916 onwards, when the majority of Germans began to long for peace regardless of the costs, the military leadership became increasingly entrenched in their demands for a Victory Peace. Something had to be gained from the war, a foreign nation defeated so it could bear the costs of it. A peace without gain would mean economic ruin for Germany.

The enormous funds that were artificially created were supposed to cover two essential demands. One, the war machinery had to be fed raw materials, manpower and infrastructure on an unprecedented scale to maintain this industrial war of attrition. Two, the civilian population at home and the enormous fighting force on the front lines had to be supplied with food and essential goods at least to a point where morale remained unaffected by rationing and shortages. The length, scale and nature

---

[*]   Figures compiled by Harold Marcuse, Professor of German History at UC Santa Barbara.

[†]   Wehler., p.202.

of conflict in the First World War made both demands impossible. Nearly half of all the German imports of raw material before the war came from overseas and so were immediately cut off by the British naval blockade. Straight after the declaration of war on 4 August 1914, the British government imposed a general trade embargo on Germany. As this 'hunger blockade' was at least in part aimed at the civilian population, it constituted a breach of international law that was even criticised by neutral nations such as the USA, where German Americans were outraged and demanded action. In addition, the blockade brought a serious disruption of the cotton trade, angering the business lobby in America, who saw no reason to take sides in a European war if it meant economic pain. The sinking of the *Lusitania* and the unrestricted submarine warfare conducted by the German navy quickly changed such reservations. Britain was thus able to set up a blockade using mines and patrols in the Channel as well as in the north between the Orkney Islands and Norway, which controlled incoming trade vessels and prevented the German navy from exiting the North Sea. With this 'remote' blockade in place, Germany was unable to obtain nearly half of its imports, which included raw materials needed for the war but also food, coffee and soap. This affected both aims of the war economy critically and thus the only solution was to make do. Supplies had to be saved wherever possible or replaced with alternative goods that could be obtained at home or from allies.

This sudden and unexpected need for economic coordination required an unprecedented degree of governmental intervention. No such suitable structures were in place in 1914. When it became apparent that the naval blockade could not be broken easily and the war in the west had bogged down into trench warfare, the transition to command economy had to be made quickly rather than thoughtfully. As early as August 1914, the

Kriegsrohstoffabteilung (KRA – War Raw Materials Department) was set up and led by Walther Rathenau, a Jewish businessman and the founder of AEG. It was a telling sign how admired he was for his economic expertise that he was trusted with such a crucial issue. Tragically, the war would sharpen anti-Semitic sentiment in Germany and his sparkling political career came to a brutal end in 1922. Driving through Berlin in his convertible motorcar on the way to the Foreign Office, he was ambushed by two members of an ultra-nationalist group called the Organisation Consul. One fired an MP 18 submachine gun at Rathenau, the other threw a grenade into his car. Rathenau was killed immediately, a tragic symbol of the radicalisation of German politics in the First World War. It is somewhat ironic that Jewish businessmen like him were blamed for the military defeat when Rathenau tried his level best to meet the increasingly ludicrous demands made by the OHL. Sodium nitrate, for example, which was used in munitions production as well as agricultural fertiliser, had previously largely been imported from Chile. Rathenau coordinated its replacement with synthetic ammonia, created through the so-called Haber-Bosch process for which Fritz Haber would eventually receive the Nobel Chemistry Prize in 1918. This was done on such a scale that the product could be widely used in war production and agriculture.

Nonetheless, there was a limit even to the most competent management, and the German war economy ran into serious supply issues after only a few months of fighting. This now made requisitioning and rationing an unpalatable necessity. Initially, some raw materials such as cotton could still be imported through Italy, but when it joined the war in 1915 on the side of the Entente powers, this supply line dried out, too. Linen and hemp were quickly planted as a replacement but were, of course, not able to cover the huge demand for cloth in such a short time. A bizarre and hugely unpopular process of forceful requisition began. Local authorities confiscated everything from underpants and bedsheets to door handles and roof tiles. Church bells and brass instruments were melted down and gold and silver jewellery forcefully taken regardless of sentimental value to their owners. This desperate and largely unsuccessful process demonstrated for all to see how much Germany was struggling to keep up in the battle of supplies with its opponents.

When Paul von Hindenburg assumed overall military command and formed the Third OHL in August 1916, it was in the midst of the unfathomable human and economic disasters of Verdun, the Somme and Brusilov. The Hindenburg Programme thus called for a transition to total war. As if a command economy had not already been created by the Enabling Act of 4 August 1914, in which the parties had surrendered all economic policy to the government, Hindenburg now demanded absolutely everything to be sacrificed. No regard whatsoever was paid to the situation of German civilians. The vast demands for coal, for example, meant that very little of what was sourced was going anywhere but the war effort. This led to such a drastic shortage of energy for German industry that electricity, and waterworks came to a grinding halt, flinging entire regions back into the Middle Ages. Steam trains needed coal and could not operate, meaning even the few supplies available did not reach their targets any more. The desperation of the military elites to get something, anything, out of the war during 1916 to 1918 led to the most severe economic crisis the country had experienced.

The final two war years were marked by an ever-widening imbalance between the economic capacity of the combatant nations. Expecting a one-front war by successful execution of the Schlieffen Plan, Germany found itself surrounded by a world of enemies in 1917. The exit of revolutionary Russia in late 1917 brought brief but unrealistic hopes that all the material effort could be flung at the Western Front. However, the reinforcement of the Western Front by a seemingly never-ending supply of American economic power brought such fancies to a crushing end. The death blow to the war economy came in October 1918, when Austria and occupied Romania fell. This dried up the supply of mineral oil, which had become a vital ingredient of industrialised warfare as engine-driven machinery and vehicles replaced horse and manpower. The supplies in German storage would have lasted a couple of months at most, but at that point the population was war-weary, the military situation hopeless and the political situation unstable.

The question of whether or not the German war economy was mismanaged has occupied historians for decades but it is a rather moot point. None of the combatant nations in 1914 was able to foresee the nature and scale of the Great War. It is true that some nineteenth-century conflicts such as the Crimean War and the American Civil War foreshadowed some of the economic devastation of modern conflict, but by 1914 they had faded into history. The Franco-Prussian War of 1870 served as the model for the German military. There were unexpected obstacles and unpleasant episodes, especially for French civilians, but in all, the war was short and economically worthwhile from a German perspective. The war of attrition that unfolded from 1914 could not have been foreseen and no amount of planning, management and economic brilliance would have made up for the material imbalance between the Central Powers and their enemies. The economic war was lost for Germany as soon as the first shot was fired in August 1914.

Suffering and Sacrifice

Peter Kollzitz was enjoying the summer holidays of 1914. The teenager was part of the popular *Wandervogel* youth movement, which rebelled against modernisation by idealising nature and pre-industrial life. He joined his friends Hans Koch, Erich Krems and Richard Noll on a hiking holiday to Norway, and he waved his mother Käthe goodbye as the ship left Wilhelmshaven. As they hiked, they sang folk songs, recited poetry by the campfire at night and enjoyed the clean air and spectacular scenery. But their peace was shattered on 1 August, when news reached them that Germany had declared war. The patriotic youngsters vowed immediately to rally to the defence of their fatherland and abruptly cancelled the rest of their holiday. When Peter returned to the family home in Berlin on 6 August, he found that his older brother Hans had already signed up to volunteer as a medic in the army, and his mother had joined the *Nationaler Frauendienst*, a women's organisation that rallied all available volunteers to help out on the home front. A black, red and white flag hung from their window for the first time. Peter was moved. He too wanted to help and do his duty. At 18 years old, he was still considered a minor and needed his father Karl's permission to join the voluntary *Landwehr* corps. On 10 August, Käthe wrote in her diary: 'In the evening Peter is asking Karl to allow him to join the ranks of the Landsturm volunteers. Karl brings up every argument he can against this. [...] All the time he looks at me silently, pleadingly, to speak for him. [...] I get up and Peter follows; we stand at the door and hug and kiss, and I plead with Karl to let Peter go.'* Eventually Herr Kollwitz gave in and Peter joined Reserve Infantry Regiment 207 as a

---

★   Translated from Käthe Kollwitz's diary.

musketeer together with his friends. After a few weeks of basic training, the boys were deemed ready. On 12 October 1914 they went to war. His mother's tattered copy of Goethe's *Faust* and a pocket chess set in his bag, Peter boarded the train to Belgium. His friend Erich Krems described what the boys found there:

> For three days we've been lying by the roadside. [...] We are now quite indifferent to the battery fire far away and nearby; we see a lot going by: furiously whipping artillery, medics, pioneers, ammunition columns, the swift cars of the General Command – everyone forwards, to battle. [...] But we have to wait and do nothing. We are the reserves. But we can feel the battle. And it could happen at any time, the call 'to the rifles', which will take us into the trenches and into the great game of the 'tightrope walker'.*

Käthe Kollwitz wrote to her son. She confessed that she was concerned for his life, but that she dealt with her fears in her art, sketching images 'to release the pressure from my heart onto the paper'. Getting no replies, her writing became increasingly emotional in tone: 'My dear boy – do you receive our postcards? It is an odd feeling to think that none of what we write ever gets to you.' And indeed Peter never read this last message. The postcard it was written on arrived back in Berlin on 30 October with the note, 'Returned to sender – dead'. Käthe Kollwitz had lost her youngest son only ten days after he had gone to war. She never recovered from her grief and her guilt. The senseless and violent way in which her boy had thrown away his life with her encouragement would haunt her for the rest of her life. Much of her

---

*   Translated from Winterberg, p. 90.

Kollwitz's first work after her son's death in 1915 depicts a mother
protectively holding an infant.

shockingly realistic drawings, sculptures and sketches in the
1920s and '30s depict a grieving mother and her dead sons,
such as her woodcut collection, titled 'War', which she completed between 1921 and 1923. During the war itself she could
not bring herself to finish a sculpture she had begun in memory

of Peter and she destroyed it in 1919.* Her initial patriotism turned into radical pacifism and she fought passionately against the government's increasingly desperate calls for recruits.

What happened to the Kollwitz family was a fate that would repeat itself millions of times and across all social strata. In total, nearly 2 million Germans would die on the front lines. Of all young German men who were between 19 and 22 when war broke out in 1914, a staggering 35 per cent would not be alive four years later when the war ended. This 'lost generation' left a gaping hole in families, communities and German society generally, and the fact that they had sacrificed their lives in vain created a collective sense of resentment and embitterment that would haunt Germany for years to come. In contrast to the glorification of the war dead in France, Great Britain and the USA, where the fallen were celebrated as war heroes who had sacrificed themselves for a greater good, German families had no such solace. They were told that they were wrong to follow the Kaiser into war, to send their sons, brothers and husbands into a doomed, imperialist venture. There would be no Armistice Day celebrations and the SPD governments of the 1920s found dealing with the war memories awkward and painful.

Already during the war itself, many, like the Kollwitzs, were abruptly torn out of their romanticised vision of the heroic struggle for the fatherland by the realities of war. Where at the beginning of August 1914 parents had dreamt of a son returning home in a neatly pressed uniform with medals on his chest and all before Christmas, in reality more and more received no answers to their postcards. Their sons lay dead and forgotten in the mud of foreign fields, or buried hastily wherever possible. Those who came home often did so with horrible

---

*   MacGregor, p.404.

disfigurements. In total over 4.2 million Germans would be injured. Painters such as Otto Dix captured scenes in Berlin and other German cities where war veterans with amputations, unable to work, were reduced to begging and homelessness. But the worst fate was reserved for the scores of men with facial injuries. The nature of the First World War made these tragically common. In August 1914, German soldiers were still sent out with the iconic spiked helmet, the *pickelhaube*. They not only made the wearer an eye-catching target in the context of trench warfare, but they were also made from leather and thus completely useless against bullets and shrapnel. In 1915, the war machine began to run out of leather and substitute helmets were made from starched felt or even paper, something that only changed in 1916 when steel helmets were slowly rolled out. In any case, all helmets left the jaw area, mouth, nose and eyes completely exposed. An exploding shell would fling red-hot pieces of metal through the air at terrible speed. Soldiers who were hit and survived were often left with ruined faces. Skin and bone grafts were not yet widely available and the best that could be done for these men was painted tin masks that would cover the gaping holes where there was once a jaw or teeth or a nose. Eating and drinking was often only possible with great difficulty, and many died of infection months or even years later. Those who survived would be shunned. Fervent patriotism began to turn into anger and resentment.

At home things looked bleak as well. The unification wars had set an example of how wars could be fought, and won, without much impact on the civilian population at home. Therefore, the militaries had done virtually no planning as regards the food supplies for the civilian population; not even rationing was deemed necessary. Only when the British naval blockade and bad harvests led to severe shortages as early as in the first war winter of 1914–15 did the General High Command begin to

Otto Dix, *War Cripples*, oil on canvas, 1920. Originally exhibited in the First International Dada Fair, Berlin.

plan for a more direct management of food production, pricing and distribution. By then it was too late, culminating in the so-called 'turnip winter' of 1916–17, which added a terrible potato blight to existing undersupply. Germans suffered from such malnutrition during the war that it is estimated that some 750,000 of them died from the consequences. In the last war years, coal, wood and oil shortages also meant that the bitter winter of 1917–18 had to be endured without adequate heating while water and electricity supplies were also breaking down, leaving the population in dark and unhygienic conditions. From the spring of 1918, the terrible Spanish flu epidemic was spreading from the trenches on the Western Front back home, where it found unresisting victims in the starving population. In Berlin alone 50,000 people died of the epidemic within the first six months of the outbreak; 350,000 more Germans fell victim to it elsewhere.

In the midst of all of this suffering and chaos, Germans were still expected to fight or work for the fatherland. All men between the ages of 20 and 45 could be requisitioned for seven years of service and only those with extremely important and specialised jobs were exempt. The government did not have to enforce this at first. The armies of volunteers were enough to overwhelm the recruitment offices.* Within twelve days in August 1914, the army had been expanded from 800,000 to 3.5 million without resistance. But as the war dragged on and death notes and crippled soldiers were sent home, enthusiasm waned accordingly. The *Hilfspflichtgesetz* of December 1916 made it compulsory for those who had not been drafted for military service to work in the war industries or wherever else they were needed. However, by that point most able-bodied men had already been drafted and only hard-to-replace specialists remained. The OHL even had to send 40,000 coal miners back home from the front lines due to the sharp decline in production that exacerbated the desperate military and civilian situation of that terrible winter.

Where possible, women were supposed to replace men in fields and factories, and the Hindenburg Programme initially foresaw a legal obligation for them to be included in the *Hilfspflichtgesetz*. Interestingly this caused so much resentment in the political class as well as the wider public that the idea was quickly dropped. Instead, women were incentivised through employment schemes and propaganda. Contrary to popular belief, this had limited impact. It is simply not the case that the First World War in Germany brought about a wave of female emancipation and that women, liberated from the yoke of their husbands, could finally break free and join the wonderful work of factory labour. True, the proportion of the

---

*   Thamer, p.35.

female workforce outside of the home grew by 12 per cent during the war, but as many studies in the 1970s and '80s have shown,[*] this was largely a restructuring rather than growth. With consumer items such as civilian clothing experiencing a rapid decline, jobs in textile production – a typical female occupation that was often conducted from home – became less viable, while male factory workers became an increasingly rare commodity and women could earn better wages there. Most 'new' women workers were thus recruited from the ranks of those who had already laboured for wages, while rural women worked the fields and mended machinery unrecognised just as they had done for generations. Male co-workers in factories were also often still disparaging rather than appreciative. With up to fourteen hours of hard physical labour a day, the work was tough and complaints such as the following from the diary of a German worker in 1918 were commonplace: 'Not a single night goes by where not at least one woman, sometimes even several, collapse at the machines.' But women were vocal and influential members of the peace movement. Brave and outspoken individuals like Käthe Kollwitz, Clara Zetkin and Rosa Luxemburg spoke for many women when they opposed the further senseless slaughter of an entire generation of young German men. Luxemburg's involvement in the peace movement, and specifically her leadership of the far-left *Spartakusbund*, would later lead to her terrible murder in January 1919. In the tumultuous post-war winter, 'Red Rosa' joined her fellow revolutionaries in an attempt to establish a socialist regime. In the process, right-wing counterrevolutionaries arrested her and questioned her under torture before she was battered unconscious with rifle butts and then shot dead. Her body was unceremoniously flung into the Landwehr

---

[*]   See for example Bajohr.

Canal in Berlin. Her bravery during and after the war remained unforgotten. Over 100,000 Berliners turned up at her funeral and to this day annual processions to her grave are held on 15 January, the day of her death.

In social terms, the First World War can only be described as traumatic for the German people. While this is also true for the French and British populations – both had suffered unprecedented casualties and in France's case huge devastation had been caused to land and property, too – Germany's psychological trauma was unique. In 1914, the nation had stood proudly as an economic and military superpower. A nation of world-leading inventors, thinkers and scientists with record living standards. Four years later, its economy, military and reputation lay in tatters. Its population was severely depleted; survivors scarred, starved and humiliated. The fall of the German Empire was devastating in its depth. All the sacrifices, hardship and loss for nothing. While the war exacerbated social divisions, with access to the black market now vital for survival and the working classes disproportionately hit by death, injury, disease and starvation, it was also strangely unifying. The trauma of the First World War can be compared to that of the Thirty Years' War, which had begun exactly 300 years earlier. A collective catastrophe that would fuel a shared sense of national defiance.

The Fall of the German Empire

'Treason!' Wilhelm exclaimed over and over again as he paced in his room at the military headquarters in Spa, Belgium. It was 9 November 1918 and at 2 p.m. he had been told that his Imperial Chancellor, Max von Baden, had announced the Kaiser's abdication two and a half hours earlier. He was sitting at his desk when the news arrived, just about to sign a document that he was indeed willing to renounce the Imperial throne, but not the Prussian one. This was a constitutional and practical impossibility and Prince Max knew that. He had sent Prussian Minister for the Interior 'Bill' Drews to the Kaiser on 1 November to convince him to abdicate, but to no avail. Eight days later, the military and political situation had become too precarious to rely on Wilhelm's whims. Decisions had to be made and Max von Baden had taken matters into his own hands. The Kaiser was outraged. Sitting in an armchair by the fireplace, he smoked one cigarette after another, brooding over his own future and that of his country. He began drafting a telegram, repeating a threat he had already made a few days earlier on the telephone, 'If you don't come to your senses in Berlin, I will lead my troops there and shoot the whole place!'* No, it would not do. He screwed up the note and threw it into the fire. He would have to confront the traitors in Berlin himself. Boarding the royal train to return to Germany, he was informed that the journey would be impossible. Local unrest had led to the seizing of many stations. The royal train would most likely be stopped and the Kaiser's life would be at risk from angry socialist agitators. Like a common refugee, Wilhelm was made to dress up in disguise and flee. The train changed course for Holland, where it was hoped that the ruling house of Orange-Nassau would allow one of their Hohenzollern relatives entry. In the early hours of 10 November, a tired and indignant Wilhelm crossed the border, arriving at his friend Count Godard van Aldenburg-Bentinck's manor shortly after. Queen Wilhelmina of the Netherlands hesitated for two more days but then resolved not to extradite Wilhelm as a war criminal. Even as pressure on her to do so mounted, she did not give

---

*   Translated from Kissel.

in. Instead she called the allied ambassadors to her palace and spelled out the rules of political asylum to them. Wilhelm was able to move to the recently renovated Huis Doorn, where he was able to live a quiet but refined life in retirement, spending an estimated 66 million marks in the first year alone. Signing his official abdication on 28 November, he cut all formal ties with Germany and had to promise not to get involved in politics ever again. While he could not stop fantasising about a restoration of Hohenzollern power, he never undertook any serious efforts in that direction. Instead, Wilhelm found some peace in the almost obsessive hobby of wood cutting, proudly counting tree trunk number 12,000 on 19 November 1919. Fittingly, this was also how his life ended. In March 1941, he collapsed in his lumberyard and never recovered. He died on 4 June at the age of 82, without having set foot in his fatherland since that fateful November of 1918.

There has long been a debate as to whether the Hohenzollern monarchy could have been salvaged. Christopher Clark maintains that 'it is plausible that the throne might have remained intact, had Wilhelm not left the capital for the general headquarters at Spa on 29 October'[*] and if he had invested as much time courting the press and public opinion as he used to. German historian Christoph Nonn, on the other hand, speaks of an 'erosion of legitimacy'[†] that had affected both royal authority and wider aristocratic supremacy since 1914. He argues that the war had accelerated this pre-existing trend and military defeat was the nail in the coffin of the old order. There can be no doubt that the First World War is the central factor in the downfall of the Hohenzollern monarchy. True, there were many among the ranks of the Social Democrats and the

---

[*]   Clark, *Wilhelm*, p.341.

[†]   Nonn, p.106.

liberals who called for a republic before 1914, but the German people on the whole still regarded the existing order as the norm. Even the prolonged and disastrous war itself was at first not attributed to Wilhelm's failings. It was his behaviour in 1917 and 1918 that damaged his standing beyond repair. While his subjects toiled, suffered and died, the Kaiser played cards with his cronies, far away from the capital. Now afraid of the public he had once so openly courted, he preferred to cocoon himself in the surreal world of his small inner circle. His only saving grace was the decision to finally sack an increasingly deranged Ludendorff on 26 October 1918. When it became increasingly obvious that the Allies would only accept something tantamount to a full surrender as the precondition for an armistice, Ludendorff suddenly declared that 'soldierly honour' would dictate a 'fight to the bitter end'. This 'Harakiri Policy'* even contained a short-lived suggestion that Wilhelm himself should dress up in battle gear and run at the enemy in an attempt to salvage his honour by dying a soldier's death in the trenches, much like so many of his people had. The dismissal of the deranged warlord gave a brief window of opportunity for the Kaiser to adjust the perception of his reign and person in posterity, but there was no possible path to holding on to monarchical rule. The Allies had made that clear. If Germany wanted peace, it needed to reform.

When Ludendorff himself had told the Kaiser on 29 September 1918 that military defeat could no longer be averted, this should have sped up armistice negotiations. The problem was that the Allies now, of course, saw no reason whatsoever to make concessions. With a seemingly never-ending supply of goods and men ready to reinforce the war effort, the USA was particularly relaxed about having to

---

*   Ibid., p.105.

prolong the war if necessary, even with the option of invading Germany itself. Faced with the complete destruction of the fatherland, the militaries finally accepted that they had to compromise and offered to accept the initial US offer based on President Woodrow Wilson's Fourteen Points. But the American note to the German government on 14 October made it abundantly clear that peace would only be possible if the 'arbitrary power' of the German monarchy were destroyed. Wilson confirmed that 'the whole process of peace will, in his judgement, depend on the definiteness and the satisfactory character of the guarantees which can be given in this fundamental matter'.* In other words there would be no peace while Wilhelm reigned and even the elites now understood reform was unavoidable. Thus, just before its demise, the German Empire was dragged, kicking and screaming, into a brief phase of genuine democracy.

As with Wilhelm's abdication, chancellor Max von Baden was the central figure in leading the reforms. Upon taking office on 1 October, he began a radical reshaping of government, pushing through reforms in weeks that the political left had demanded for decades. On 26 October, the package of legislation was passed by a majority consisting of SPD, Centre and liberal members of the Reichstag. These October reforms put parliament at the heart of government, making the chancellor responsible to it rather than to the Kaiser. Decisions of war and peace would in future be made by Reichstag and Bundesrat. Prussia had also abolished its hated three-tier voting system and the constituencies were redrawn to represent more fairly the urban proletariat in elections. With the abdication of the Kaiser on 9 November, the process of democratisation had gone far

---

*   'Correspondence Between the United States and Germany Regarding an Armistice', p.89.

enough for the Allies to agree to an armistice and the guns finally fell silent two days later.

It is unlikely that this reluctantly professed love for democratic reform by the German elites alone would have sufficed to convince the Americans and their even more sceptical European allies France and Britain that they were now dealing with a peaceful Germany. The so-called 'German Revolution' in November played a key role in this process. On 29 October 1918, the same day that the Kaiser fled to Spa in Belgium and seemed to abandon them, a further sign of their utter contempt for ordinary people was sent by the elites. Despite their passive role in the war since the skirmishes of 1915–16, the commanders of the German fleet decided that their hour had come. Without consulting the government in Berlin, the OHL or the Kaiser, they ordered the fleet at Kiel harbour to sail out and meet the Royal Navy for a last stand. This was tantamount to a suicide mission and the angry and war-weary sailors were in no mood for misguided and self-destructive heroism. They mutinied in spectacular fashion, not giving the authorities an inch. Even when the leaders were arrested, their comrades raided the military prisons and liberated them on 3 November. Law and order broke down, and the old dreams of revolution seemed to be coming true for many socialists. A wave of revolutionary fervour swept through German cities and in many places Soviet-model workers' councils replaced local authorities. Train stations, post offices and news agencies were occupied as the elites feared a Russian-style reckoning. SPD and USPD reluctantly attempted to take leadership of the somewhat intimidating genie they had been trying to let out of the bottle for so long. As it turned out, both the elites and the extreme wing of the socialist movement were wrong to think a genuine revolution was imminent. What drove sailors, soldiers and workers onto the streets was not their desire to build a classless utopia, it was war-weariness, hunger and despair. Any government that could make peace could end their anger. Max von Baden and moderate SPD leader Friedrich Ebert understood this when they conspired to force the Kaiser's abdication and declare Germany a republic.

On 9 November, the situation came to a head. Prince Max knew that, as a member of the aristocracy, he would simply not be suitable to lead a government that would have to convince the German public and the Allies that things were genuinely changing. In an unconstitutional move, he handed his powers as chancellor directly to Friedrich Ebert. The SPD leader seemed the ideal compromise candidate. A level-headed, moderate and well-respected proponent of constitutional monarchy, he was expected to provide a bridge between the elites and the masses. To put the leader of the largest political party at the helm of the new regime would also demonstrate to the Allies that they were now dealing with a genuine democracy. Ebert's good friend and fellow SPD man Philipp Scheidemann announced the news to the German public. Speaking from a window of the Reichstag building in Berlin, he told the assembled masses that the Kaiser had abdicated and that Germany was now a republic. Fearing that the revolution was slipping through their fingers while the moderates of the reform-minded SPD were taking charge, the radical socialists of the *Spartakusbund* had to do something. Their leader, Karl Liebknecht, who had been the only MP to vote against further war credits in December 1914 and had then spent much of the war in prison for high treason, decided to address the Berliners as well. Two hours after Scheidemann's declaration of a 'democratic republic', Liebknecht stepped on to a balcony of Berlin Palace and pronounced the establishment of a 'free socialist republic' to a bewildered audience.

These two contrasting visions of Germany's post-war future epitomise the problems that the spectacular demise of the

German Empire had brought about. When the dust of perpetual conflict settled, what was revealed was a nation that was still insecure, disunited and unsure of its political identity. The only thing that most Germans could agree on was what they did not want: Wilhelm, war and the misery both had inflicted on them. The German Empire did not fall to visions of democracy or socialism. Neither was it brought down by the German people or the Allies. The system fell because it was flawed from the outset, built on foundations of war, not fraternity. The maintenance of national unity required a diet of conflict, the constant hunger for which grew until catastrophe loomed in 1914. The German Empire had come full circle. It ended where it had started: in blood and iron.

CONCLUSIONS: THE END?

This very day forty-eight years ago, on January 18, 1871, the German Empire was proclaimed by an army of invasion in the Chateau at Versailles. [...] born in injustice, it has ended in opprobrium. You are assembled in order to repair the evil that it has done and to prevent a recurrence of it.*

These were the words with which French President Poincaré opened the Paris Peace Conference, reminding the assembled representatives of over thirty nations what they had come to do. The chosen date and location for the occasion were highly symbolic. France had invited the world to not only right the wrongs of 1914–18, but also those of 1871. Prime Minister Georges Clemenceau had already reserved the Palace of Versailles as the venue for the signing of the peace treaty before he even knew what it would eventually say. Whatever else came out of the conference, France must never again be exposed to 'the periodic tide of the same invasions'.† The 77-year-old Clemenceau had seen

---

*   Raymond Poincaré, 'Welcoming Address at the Paris Peace Conference', 18 January 1919.
†   Ibid.

it twice in his lifetime and would fight tooth and nail to destroy Germany – at Versailles, the very place where it was created.

However, Germany would not be destroyed in 1919. In nearly five decades, the new nation state had established itself in the economic, political and psychological fabric of Europe and the world in a way that made it neither desirable nor feasible to eradicate it overnight. Exasperated with French sentimentality on the issue, the USA and Britain gave in to some of Clemenceau's demands. The British Prime Minister Lloyd George later complained: 'I never wanted to hold the Conference in his bloody capital [...] but the old man wept and protested so much that we gave way.'* However, a line was firmly drawn where the complete dismantling of the German nation state was concerned. Nonetheless, Germany lost a lot of land, such as the inevitable restoration of Alsace and Lorraine as French provinces, but also in the establishment of Poland as an independent state, carved out of German and Russian territory. Northern Schleswig was given to Denmark, other areas went to Belgium and Lithuania. In all Germany lost 6.5 million people and 27,000 square miles of land, which amounted to 10 and 13 per cent losses compared to pre-war levels respectively. This caused a simmering resentment that would plague the young German democracy rising from the ashes of war. Nonetheless, it was a far cry from the French plan to dismantle the nation state completely. Encouraging secession movements in the Catholic southern states and Rhineland, it was hoped that a three-part split along the rivers Rhine, Main and Oder could be achieved so that the eastern part went to Poland while the south and Rhine regions became separate German confederations respectively. The eternal French fear that Germany had two for every one thing France had – be that people, land, troops or resources

---

*   Quoted from MacMillan, p.35.

– would thus be alleviated. The war had destroyed the Tsarist, Ottoman and Austro-Hungarian Empires, all of which had long histories and traditions. So surely the young German Empire would fall apart under a bit of pressure? If war and victory were the glue that held it together, peace and humiliation would quickly dissolve the fragile union.

The French did their utmost to encourage separatist clamour on the left side of the Rhine in particular, as it was occupied by Allied troops. There was indeed much anti-Prussian sentiment there and the 'German Revolution' in the industrial Ruhr region had been particularly hostile towards Hohenzollern overlordship. However, as with the Rhine crisis of 1840, anything that smacked of French annexation of this German region brought back collective memories of Napoleonic oppression. Furthermore, the hated Kaiser was gone in any case. Most Rhinelanders felt the German defeat acutely and found French revanchism unpalatable. The south also did not comply with French hopes. It was true that the region was hostile towards Prussian and Hohenzollern power in Berlin, and the German Revolution in Bavaria was accompanied by calls for secession. On 8 November 1918, a day before Wilhelm's abdication, socialist Kurt Eisner declared Bavaria a 'Free Republic' that never wanted anything to do with a war caused by 'a small horde of mad Prussian military' men. However, working with the capitalist French did not appeal to Bavarian socialists either. When it became apparent that a union with Catholic Austria was unacceptable to the Allies, the southern states had nowhere to go and remained in the German union, satisfied with the federalism that allowed them a degree of self-government.

What had happened in the forty-eight years since the creation of Germany, which made the concept of nation so real that secession from it remained the pipe dream of a few extremists? How had Rhinelanders, Bavarians and Prussians turned into Germans? Why did Catholics not seek the opportunity to finally leave the oppression of the Protestant majority? Why did the south not try to distance themselves from the warmongering Prussians? The answer is complex. Education, secularisation and conscription certainly all played a role. The huge population growth that Germany had seen in this time meant that the majority of Germans were young. They had never experienced anything but a nation state and grew up glorifying the unification wars and Bismarck as the founding father. They went through two or three years of military service together, travelled freely across the German lands to flock to the cities and worked side by side with fellow countrymen from different states and regions. Interconfessional marriages were on the rise, while science replaced religion as a compass to navigating life. Germans had taken pride together in their colonial empire. They had developed a communal liking for coffee and the resulting cafe culture added a new dimension to social life that was singularly German, not regional. They had cheered German shipbuilding, engineering and scientific breakthroughs. They had a national anthem, a flag as well as national heroes and a world-class economy of which to be proud.

All of this was compounded by the collective catastrophe of the First World War. A nation whose men had fought in grim camaraderie in the trenches, whose women and children had toiled, starved and suffered at home, had experienced a shared trauma that bound it together. The despair and humiliation of 1918 and 1919 was met with shared defiance and anger. What Bismarck and Wilhelm had created now seemed a golden age from the perspective of the darkness of defeat. It is no coincidence that 'surrogate Kaiser' Hindenburg would not only remain unblemished in the eyes of many Germans, but also be elected as President of their new republic in 1925 following the death of Friedrich Ebert. Where people associated the Imperial regime with economic prosperity, national pride and military glory, the post-war republic began with hunger, humiliation and defeat. Suddenly the political strife of the pre-war years seemed petty and insignificant compared to the suffering that followed. It was not the cry for democracy that had shaped, moulded and marked the German national character but the shared experiences of its people.

The First World War had become a terrible milestone on Germany's path to nationhood. Instead of destroying the defensive nationalism that Bismarck and Wilhelm had cultivated, it augmented it. The blood and iron paid this time far exceeded that of the unification wars five decades earlier and the effect was correspondingly potent. The war brought the structures of the German Empire down – its crown, its borders, its military – but Bismarck's legacy would live on. Against the contrast of the dark times to come, the German Empire became an idealised image, perfectly preserved in the still, golden amber of national memory.

BIBLIOGRAPHY

Books

Andrian-Werburg, V. (1843). *Österreich und seine Zukunft*. 3 ed. Hamburg: Hoffmann.

Bajohr, S. (1984). *Die Hälfte der Fabrik: Geschichte der Frauenarbeit in Deutschland 1914 bis 1945*. Marburg: Verlag Arbeiterbewegung U. Gesellschaftswiss.

Bew, J. (2015). *Realpolitik: A History*. Oxford: Oxford University Press.

Bry, G. (1960). *Wages in Germany*. Princeton, NJ: Princeton University Press.

Carr, W. (2010). *A History of Germany, 1815–1990*. London; New York: Bloomsbury Academic.

Charles River Editors (2018). *The Austro-Prussian War and Franco-Prussian War: The History of the Wars that Led to Prussia's Unification of Germany*. Charles River Editors.

Clark, C.M. (2007). *Iron Kingdom: The Rise and Downfall of Prussia, 1600–1947*. Cambridge, Mass.; London: Belknap.

Clark, C.M. (2014). *Kaiser Wilhelm II*. London: Routledge.

Egelhaaf, G. and Bedey, B. (2011). *Theobald von Bethmann Hollweg der fünfte Reichskanzler*. Hamburg: Severus-Verl.

Epkenhans, M., Gerhard Paul Gross and Burkhard Köster (2011). *Preussen: Aufstieg und Fall einer Grossmacht*. Darmstadt: Wissenschaftliche Buchgesellschaft.

Eyck, E. (1968). *Bismarck and the German Empire*. New York: Norton.

Fulbrook, M. (2019). *A Concise History of Germany*. Cambridge, UK; New York, USA: Cambridge University Press.

Hawes, J.M. (2019). *The Shortest History of Germany: From Julius Caesar to Angela Merkel: A Retelling for Our Times*. New York: The Experiment.

Herre, F. and Verlag Kiepenheuer & Witsch (2017). *Kaiser Wilhelm II. Monarch zwischen den Zeiten*. Köln: Kiepenheuer & Witsch.

Kent, G.O. (1978). *Bismarck and his Times*. Carbondale Edwardsville: Southern Illinois University Press.

Kitchen, M. (2012). *A History of Modern Germany, 1800 to the Present*. Chichester, West Sussex, UK: Wiley-Blackwell.

Klußmann, U. and Mohr, J. (2016). *Das Kaiserreich Deutschland unter preußischer Herrschaft: von Bismarck bis Wilhelm II*. München: Goldmann [Hamburg] Spiegel-Buchverlag.

Langer, W.L. (1977). *European Alliances and Alignments, 1871–1890*. Westport, Conn: Greenwood Press.

MacGregor, N. (2017). *Germany: Memories of a Nation*. New York: Vintage Books.

Maclean, R. (2014). *Berlin: City of Imagination*. London: Weidenfeld & Nicolson.

Macmillan, M. (2005). *Peacemakers: The Paris Conference of 1919 and its Attempt to End War*. London: John Murray.

Massie, R.K. (2007). *Dreadnought: Britain, Germany, and the Coming of the Great War*. London: Vintage.

Mitchell, A. (2006). *The Great Train Race: Railways and the Franco-German Rivalry, 1815–1914*. New York: Berghahn Books.

Nonn, C. (2015). *Bismarck: ein Preusse und sein Jahrhundert*. München: C.H. Beck.

Nonn, C. (2017). *Das deutsche Kaiserreich: von der Gründung bis zum Untergang*. München: C.H. Beck.

Palmer, A. (1978). *Bismarck*. Bergisch Gladbach: Bastei-Lübbe.

Pflanze, O. (1997). *Bismarck 1. Der Reichsgründer*. München: C.H. Beck.

Pflanze, O. (2014). *Bismarck and the Development of Germany, vol. II, The Period of Consolidation, 1871–1880*. Princeton, NJ: Princeton University Press.

Prutsch, M.J. (2019). *Caesarism in the Post-Revolutionary Age*. London: Bloomsbury.

Rischbieter, J. (2011). *Mikro-Ökonomie der Globalisierung: Kaffee, Kaufleute und Konsumenten im Kaiserreich 1870–1914*. Köln Etc.: Böhlau, Cop.

Robinson, D.H. (1994). *The Zeppelin in Combat: A History of the German Naval Airship Division, 1912–1918*. Atglen, Pa: Schiffer Military/ Aviation History.

Bibliography

Rochau, L. (1972). *Grundsätze der Realpolitik: Angewendet auf die staatlichen Zustände Deutschlands.* Frankfurt A.M.: Ullstein.

Röhl, J.C.G. (2014). *Kaiser Wilhelm II, 1859–1941: A Concise Life.* Cambridge: Cambridge University Press.

Schwibbe, M.H. (2008). *Zeit reise: 1200 jahre leben in Berlin.* Berlin: Zeit Reise.

Simms, B. (2014). *Europe: The Struggle for Supremacy, 1453 to the Present.* London: Penguin Books.

Stauff, P. and Ekkehard, E. (1929). *Sigilla veri: [Ph. Stauff's Semi-Kürschner]; Lexikon der Juden, -Genossen und -Gegner aller Zeiten und Zonen, insbesondere Deutschlands, der Lehren, Gebräuche, Kunstgriffe und Statistiken der Juden sowie ihrer Gaunersprache, Trugnamen, Geheimbünde. 3, Hochmann bis Lippold.* Erfurt: Bodung.

Steinberg, J. (2013). *Bismarck: A Life.* Oxford: Oxford University Press.

Stolberg-Wernigerode, O. (1972). *Neue deutsche Biographie. [9]. Neunter Band, Hess-Hüttig.* Berlin: Duncker & Humblot. C.

Stürmer, M. (2000). *The German Empire, 1870–1918.* New York: Modern Library.

Taylor, A.J.P. (1979). *The Course of German History: A Survey of the Development of Germany Since 1815.* New York: Paragon.

Thamer, H.U. (2017). *Der Erste Weltkrieg: Europa zwischen Euphorie und Elend.* Berlin: Palm Verlag.

Ullrich, V. (2014). *Die nervöse Großmacht: 1871–1918; Aufstieg und Untergang des deutschen Kaiserreichs.* Frankfurt A.M.: Fischer.

Ullrich, V. (2015). *Bismarck.* London: Haus Publishing Limited.

Verhey, J. (2006). *The Spirit of 1914: Militarism, Myth and Mobilization in Germany.* Cambridge; New York: Cambridge University Press.

Vogt, M. (1991). *Deutsche Geschichte von den Anfängen bis zur Wiedervereinigung.* Stuttgart Metzler.

Walser Smith, H. (2014). *German Nationalism and Religious Conflict: Culture, Ideology, Politics, 1870–1914.* Princeton, NJ: Princeton University Press.

Wehler, H.-U. (1997). *The German Empire: 1871–1918.* Oxford; New York: Berg, Cop.

Weintraub, S. and Mazal Holocaust Collection (1993). *Disraeli: A Biography.* New York: Truman Talley Books/Dutton.

Wende, P. (2005). *A History of Germany.* New York: Palgrave Macmillan.

Winterberg, Y. and Winterberg, S. (2015). *Kollwitz: die Biografie.* München: Bertelsmann.

Winzen, P. (2013). *Reichskanzler Bernhard von Bülow: mit Weltmachtphantasien in den Ersten Weltkrieg: eine politische Biographie.* Regensburg: Verlag Friedrich Pustet.

Articles

Baumgart, W., 'Chlodwig zu Hohenlohe-Schillingsfürst', *Die deutschen Kanzler. Von Bismarck bis Kohl*, vol. 2, pp.55–67.

Brophy, J., 'The Rhine Crisis of 1840 and German Nationalism: Chauvinism, Skepticism, and Regional Reception', *The Journal of Modern History*, vol. 85, pp.1–35.

Chisholm, H., 'Rhine Province', *Encyclopædia Britannica*, vol. 23, pp.242–43.

Hatfield, D., 'Kulturkampf: The Relationship of Church and State and the Failure of German Political Reform', *Journal of Church and State*, vol. 23, pp.465–84.

Heilbronner, H., 'The Russian Plague of 1878–79', *Slavic Review*, vol. 21, pp.89–112.

LeMO. 'Lebendiges Museum Online'. *Deutsches Historisches Museum*, www.dhm.de/lemo (Accessed, 25 August 2020).

Kissel, T., 'Der schrille Zwangspensionär', *Spektrum – Die Woche*, vol. 5/2019.

Kretzschmar, U., 'Foreword', *German Colonialism: Fragments Past and Present*, pp.10–11.

Mork, G., 'Bismarck and the "Capitulation" of German Liberalism', *The Journal of Modern History*, vol. 43, pp.59–75.

Paret, P., 'Anton von Werner's "Kaiserproklamation in Versailles"', *Kunst als Geschichte. Kultur und Politik von Menzel bis Fontane*, pp.193–210.

Reichling, H., 'Das Duell', *Transcript of a Lecture,* www.reichling-zweibruecken.de/duell.htm (Accessed, 25 August 2020).

Röhl, J., 'The Kaiser and his Court', *History Review,* vol. 25, September 1996.

Schröder, W., 'Die Entwicklung der Arbeitszeit im sekundären Sektor in Deutschland 1871 bis 1913', *Technikgeschichte*, vol. 47, pp.252–302.

Shlomo, A., 'Hegel and Nationalism', *The Review of Politics,* vol. 24, pp.461–84.

Snyder, L., 'Nationalistic Aspects of the Grimm Brothers' Fairy Tales', *The Journal of Social Psychology.* vol. 33, pp.209–23.

Stapleton, F., 'The Unpredictable Dynamo: Germany's Economy, 1870–1918', *History Review,* Issue 44.

Statista. 'Made-in-Country-Index (Mici) 2017 Report', de.statista.com/
page/Made-In-Country-Index (Accessed, 25 August 2020).

Stern, F., 'Money, Morals, and the Pillars of Bismarck's Society', *Central
European History*, vol. 3, pp.49–72.

Wassermann, A., 'Wildwest im Ruhrgebiet', *Der Spiegel*, vol. 03/2013.

Sources and Documents

Friedrich Wilhelm III, 'To My People' (17 March 1813). Source of
English translation: Robinson, J., *Readings in European History, A
collection of extracts from the sources chosen with the purpose of illustrating
the progress of culture in Western Europe since the German Invasions*,
vol. II, pp.522–23.

Otto von Bismarck, 'Blood and Iron Speech' (20 September 1862).
Source of English translation: Riemer, J., *Otto von Bismarck, Reden
1847–1869* [Speeches, 1847–1869], vol. 10, pp.139–40.

Wilhelm Camphausen, *Die Erstürmung der Insel Alsen durch die Preußen
1864* [The Attack on the Isle of Also by the Prussians 1864].
Düsseldorf, 1866. Oil on canvas. Held in Deutsches Historisches
Museum, Berlin.

Karl Marx. 'Communist Manifesto' (February 1848). 1992 Reprint. *The
Communist Manifesto*. Oxford: Oxford University Press.

Otto von Bismarck, 'Kissingen Dictation' (1877). Source of English
translation: Hamerow, T.S.(ed.), *The Age of Bismarck: Documents and
Interpretations*. New York: Harper & Row, 1973, pp.269–72.

Richard Wagner, 'What is German?' (1865/1878). Source of English
translation: Ellis, W., *Richard Wagner's Prose Works*, vol. 4, Art and
Politics, 2 ed. London: William Reeves, 1912, pp.149–69.

Max Weber, 'Reflections on Co-operation between the National
Liberals and Bismarck during the 1860s and 1870s' (May 1918).
Source of English translation: Lassman, P. and Speirs, R., *Max Weber,
Political Writings*. Cambridge: Cambridge University Press, 1994,
pp.137–40.

Kaiser Wilhelm II, 'Decree of February 4, 1890 to the Reich Chancellor'.
Reichs- und Staatsanzeiger [Reich and State Gazette], No.34 (5
February 1890). Original German text reprinted in Ernst Rudolf
Huber, ed., *Dokumente zur Deutschen Verfassungsgeschichte* [Documents
on German Constitutional History], 3 rev. ed., vol. 2, 1851–1900.
Stuttgart: Kohlhammer, 1986, pp.510–11. Translation: Erwin Fink.

Otto von Bismarck, 'Letter of Resignation' (18 March 1890). A portion
of this translation was taken from Louis L. Snyder, ed., *Documents of*

German History. New Brunswick, NJ: Rutgers University Press, 1958, pp.266–68. Passages omitted from Snyder's anthology were translated by Erwin Fink for *German History in Documents and Images* and added to Snyder's translation. Original German text printed in *Otto von Bismarck, Die gesammelten Werke* [Collected Works], ed. Gerhard Ritter and Rudolf Stadelmann, Friedrichsruh ed., 15 vols, vol. 6c, no. 440, Berlin, 1924–1935, p.435ff.

Bernhard von Bülow, 'Germany's 'Place in the Sun' (1897).
Stenographische Berichte über die Verhandlungen des Reichstags [Stenographic Reports of Reichstag Proceedings]. IX LP, 5 Session, Vol. 1, Berlin, 1898, p.60. Original German text also reprinted in Rüdiger vom Bruch and Björn Hofmeister, eds., *Kaiserreich und Erster Weltkrieg 1871–1918* [Wilhlemine Germany and the First World War 1871–1918]. Deutsche Geschichte in Quellen und Darstellung, edited by Rainer A. Müller, vol. 8. Stuttgart: P. Reclam, 2000, pp.268–70. Translation: Adam Blauhut.

Chamberlain, Houston Stewart, 'Foundations of the nineteenth century' (1910). London; New York: J. Lane, 1911.

Kaiser Wilhelm II, 'Hun Speech' (1900). In Manfred Görtemaker, *Deutschland im 19. Jahrhundert. Entwicklungslinien* [Germany in the Nineteenth Century. Paths in Development]. Opladen, 1996. Schriftenreihe der Bundeszentrale für politische Bildung, vol. 274, p.357. Translation: Thomas Dunlap.

Kaiser Wilhelm II, 'Speech from the Balcony of the Royal Palace' (1 August 1914). Source of English translation: Kriegs-Rundschau I, p.43. Original German text reprinted in Wolfdieter Bihl, ed., *Deutsche Quellen zur Geschichte des Ersten Weltkrieges* [German Sources on the History of the First World War]. Darmstadt, 1991, p.49. Translation: Jeffrey Verhey.

Kaiser Wilhelm II, 'Speech from the Balcony of the Royal Palace' (6 August 1914). Source: Gilbert Krebs und Bernhard Poloni, *Volk, Reich und Nation. 1806–1918*. Pia, 1994, p.237.

Kaiser Wilhelm II, 'Speech to the Reichstag' (4 August 1914). Source: Friedrich Wilhelm Purlitz et al., eds., *Deutscher Geschichtskalender*, vol. 2, Leipzig 1914, p.47.

Hugo Haase, 'Speech to the Reichstag' (4 August 1914). Source: Gilbert Krebs und Bernhard Poloni, *Volk, Reich und Nation. 1806–1918*. Pia, 1994, p.239.

Hugo Haase, 'Social Democratic Party Statement on the Outbreak of the War' (4 August 1914), in *Verhandlungen des Reichstags* [Proceedings of the Reichstag], XIII. LP., II. Sess., 1914, Bd. 306, pp.8 ff. Original

German text reprinted in Ernst Rudolf Huber, *Dokumente zur deutschen Verfassungsgeschichte* [Documents on German Constitutional History]. 2 volumes. Stuttgart: Kohlhammer Verlag, 1961, vol. 2, pp.456–57. Translation: Jeffrey Verhey.

UK Parliament, 'Taxation during the First World War'. In: www.parliament.uk/about/living-heritage/transformingsociety/private-lives/taxation/overview/firstworldwar (accessed on 25 August 2020).

Harold Marcuse, 'Historical Dollar-to-Marks Currency Conversion'. In: marcuse.faculty.history.ucsb.edu/projects/currency.htm (accessed 25 August 2020)

Käthe Kollwitz, 'Diary Entry'. Source: Grober, U., 'Das kurze Leben des Peter Kollwitz', *DIE ZEIT*, 48/1996.

Woodrow Wilson, 'Correspondence Between the United States and Germany Regarding an Armistice.' (1918). Source: *The American Journal of International Law*, vol. 13, no. 2, 1919, pp.85–96.

Raymond Poincaré, 'Welcoming Address at the Paris Peace Conference' (18 January 1919). Source: *Records of the Great War*, vol. VII, ed. Charles F. Horne, National Alumni, 1923.

INDEX